GUIDANCE FROM SI

The republication of this book has been n
support of the following patrons:

Anonymous
Anonymous (Kent)
Sue Baker
P.F. Baker
Edward W. Benstead
Geoffrey Clarke
Anne Elizabeth Clay
Joan Cooke
Marie S. Davies
Olive and Alwyn Elliott
Rev. John A. Findlay
Rita Gorman
Gladys Holloway
Bob Huber
Dr and Mrs Nassif Isaac
P.A. Kay
Kenneth Mitchell
Mr and Mrs J.R.Y. MacQuarrie
Joe Murphy
Irene Newbury
Laurie O'Leary
T.W. Plumtree
A.H. Quesnel
William Richardson
Ted Ruffell
Irene Scanlon
R.J. Silver
Thomas Siney
L.A. Sterns
D.B. Stephenson
Doris Stokes
Betty Stubbs
Dudley C. Taylor
Brendon and June Totty
Peter R. Watson
J.C. Wilkins
R.P. Watkins
Betty Hepburn (in gratitude to Arthur and Kitty Simpson, MSNU)

GUIDANCE FROM SILVER BIRCH

Edited by
ANNE DOOLEY

PSYCHIC PRESS
20 Earlham Street
London WC2H 9LW

First published 1966
This edition 1986

ISBN 0 85384 066 0

Printed in Great Britain by
WBC Print Ltd, Bristol

CONTENTS

PROLOGUE

YOURS is a changing world where man is on the march towards freedom. Man has largely thrown overboard ancient shibboleths, creeds, ritual, the letter of the law and dry theology that imprisons souls.

Because of the tremendous upheaval of elemental forces being unleashed man is ready for the truths of the spirit which can guide him.

He does not trust the old because it is old. He has seen the world turning upside down in his own generation and has no respect for those who have become almost acidulated in their constant lip-service to doctrines which inwardly they do not accept.

Because of that there are thrusting, questing, eager souls in your world today, searching for that which will supply the answers to the problems that are the inevitable concomitants of present-day happenings.

The future does not belong to the conventional theologians. They have nothing to offer. The future belongs to those truths of the spirit which can satisfy the mind and the soul of all those who yearn to know.

SILVER BIRCH

Chapter One

SILVER BIRCH AND HIS MEDIUM

Over forty years ago, an argumentative, clever young man, whose own volubility as the eighteen-year-old secretary of a literary debating society had landed him into an unanticipated investigation of Spiritualism, mockingly went to his first seance in an East London tenement.

Unimpressed by the subsequent home circle proceedings, he laughed when entranced sitters temporarily became the mouthpieces for Red Indian, African and Chinese guides. Incredulous, he lightly dismissed a sitter's rebuke, "You, too, will be doing this before long," but the remark was to prove prophetic.

Halfway through the sceptic's second attendance at the humble circle, he found himself apologising to his companions for having "dropped off to sleep". To his astonishment he was told: "You have been a Red Indian while in trance. Your guide gave his name. He said he had been training you for years, having chosen you before your birth. He also said that before long you will be speaking on Spiritualist platforms."

Again he laughed, this time not quite so light-heartedly. At subsequent seances he continued to be entranced by the unknown Red Indian who at the beginning could barely string a few words of English together.

The young man was Maurice Barbanell. His guide was later named Silver Birch. Both were destined to become well known in contrasting but indissolubly linked spheres of activity—the medium as a skilled propagandist, author and editor; his guide as a spirit teacher whose eloquence over the years has won for him, in the words of Hannen Swaffer, "more followers than any earthly preacher".

He spoke authoritatively, for to this day the home circle of which Silver Birch is the guide is known as the Hannen Swaffer home circle. Also, in his own long career as an outstanding polemical journalist—the title of "The Pope of Fleet Street" was well earned—he had frequently savoured with a connoisseur's delight the finest flights of earthly oratory, expressed by such masters of the art as Keir Hardie, Philip Snowden, Lord Samuel, Lady Bonham-Carter, Lloyd George, Sir Winston Churchill and Archbishop Temple.

The secret of the Barbanell-Silver Birch psychic partnership was kept for over twenty years. As editor of *Psychic News*, and later *Two Worlds*, Barbanell had wisely insisted that while the teachings of his guide deserved the widest circulation in print—it was Swaffer who first urged their publication—they should stand or fall on their own merits. The fact that he was the medium for Silver Birch was not publicly revealed until a memorable *Two Worlds* article was written by Barbanell on August 24, 1957.

Of Silver Birch Swaffer has told us: "He is not a Red Indian. Who he is we do not know. We assume that he used the name of the spirit through whose astral body he expressed himself, it being impossible for the high vibration of the spiritual realm to which he belongs to manifest except through some other instrument. 'One day I will tell you who I am,' he told us. 'I had to come in the form of a humble Indian to win your love and devotion, not by the use of any high-sounding name, but to prove myself by the truth of what I taught. That is the law'."

Answering critics who asked, "How do you know all this teaching does not come from the medium's subconscious mind?" Swaffer pointed out that in vital respects the two personalities contradicted each other. Whereas, for example, Silver Birch teaches reincarnation, Barbanell eschews it, yet in trance, confounds his own conscious arguments.

Silver Birch has also provided other evidence through the years that he is indeed an independent being and not a "secondary personality" of the medium, an assertion favoured by perplexed researchers. On one occasion, for example, he told Barbanell's wife, Sylvia, that at a subsequent Estelle Roberts voice seance he would speak through the trumpet and repeat certain words she would have good reason to recall. The promise was strictly fulfilled. Barbanell, who was also among those present, had the thrill of hearing his guide speaking in direct voice.

The eighteenth-century French writer, Georges-Louis Leclerc De Buffon, has declared, "Style is the man himself." If this literary dictum be accepted the case rests proven, not only in relation to personality traits, but, above all, in the manner of his teaching. Indeed Barbanell, in a personal tribute to Silver Birch's teachings, which he described as an outstanding example of "spirit alchemy", once told his readers:

"As one who spends the whole of his working life in writing, I can appreciate that the faculty of being able to deliver, week after week, words of wisdom, full of eloquent simplicity, in this spontaneous fashion, is in itself evidence of supernormality. Like other journalists who live by their pen, I know that simple English is the most difficult to write. I know how you have to polish and repolish, alter words, delete others, change sentences, consult the dictionary and the thesaurus, before you are satisfied. Yet here is a 'dead' man who, without hesitation, can produce perfect prose. Everything he says is full of common sense, inspiring, uplifting and ennobling. Silver Birch's words glisten like diamonds. I salute a master of English, a great literary craftsman whom I have grown to love and admire."

Similarly, Edmund Bentley, one of South Africa's leading Spiritualists, in his book, *These Chariots of Fire*, has described the difference between Silver Birch and his medium as "startling". The contrast, he wrote, was most pronounced in speech and oratory. Bentley wrote:

"Barbanell is a competent public speaker. Long familiarity with the public platform, with banquet and with hustings, with meetings at which the audience has numbered thousands, has given him a command of words, the ability to tell a witty story and, above all, to present a case in the manner of a court-room barrister.

"But Silver Birch wipes all this clean from the human slate. He brings a grandeur and authority, compound of that higher realm of simplicity and love which has the hallmark of kingship. His mighty range of description, his immaculate choice of words and his sheer silver, glowing oratory combine to prove, if any proof were needed, that here is another being, a visitor from the realms of spirit, one who has taken over the earthly vessel and filled it with an authentic cornucopia, distinct, individual and apart."

Describing the slow evolution of complete trance control, Barbanell tells us it took years before he achieved complete unawareness of what was said: "At first I was conscious of every word uttered, even though sometimes I appeared to be either standing a few feet away from my body or suspended a few feet above it. During this period, the spirit entity gained a growing mastery over the English language, the original guttural accent gradually being replaced with a pleasant but deeper sounding voice than my own.

"So far as I am concerned, trance is a willing surrender. I compose myself, try to make myself passive and mentally offer myself, praying that the highest, best and the purest that are possible shall come through me. Then an unusual feeling of warmth steals over me. This I have experienced occasionally in my normal life. To me it is an indication of spirit presence. It is not heat in the thermometer sense, for I am sure that this instrument would not register anything more than my normal bodily temperature. Soon I feel that my breathing is becoming heavily rhythmic and even stertorous. Gradually I lose awareness of my surroundings and appear to be enveloped in a comforting kind of blanket and then 'I' have gone. Where 'I' have gone to I do not know. Perhaps, here or hereafter, I shall find out.

"I am told that the trance is achieved by the guide blending his aura with mine and then taking control of my subconscious mind. The awakening is a process that reverses the entry into trance. Usually, however warm the room is, there is a curious feeling of coldness in my lower limbs. Sometimes I know that my own emotional make-up must have been utilised, for there is a feeling almost as if I have shed tears.

"However long the trance state may last, I always awaken refreshed, no matter how tired I may have been beforehand. All I seem to require to achieve normality is a drink of some cold water which I also always have soon after the seance begins. A busy life has often meant that I go straight from the hurly-burly to the seance room, but however exhausting or stimulating the day has been it seems to make no difference to the trance state. I have been surprised on occasions, feeling so tired that it seemed purposeless to have a sitting. Yet the results have been up to their usual standard. Experience has taught me to avoid heavy meals for as long as possible before the sitting as these seem to produce a clogging effect. In opposition to what sceptics say, I find that trance mediumship functions better when nothing is known about visitors who attend the seance. Any knowledge about them presents an obstacle to a clear channel."

My own first attendance at the Silver Birch circle on an autumn evening in 1963 proved memorable, not least because it provided a fascinating first glimpse of physical phenomena. Including the six regular members of the circle, we were about a dozen in number. The atmosphere was relaxed and friendly. The seance was held in the attractive book-lined living-room of the medium's pleasant first-floor flat, situated in a tree-shaded street in one of London's inner ring suburbs.

I had heard that a "rocking table" usually initiated the sittings of the Hannen Swaffer circle, but hearing is one thing, seeing entirely another. Did not the twitching legs of dead frogs drying on an Italian balcony in the sun, observed with accidental closeness by a brilliant scientist, help usher in the age of electricity?

For me the commonplace began to crash in ruins at my feet when, placing the tips of my fingers side by side with those of my companions on the surface of the small wooden seance table, I not only observed but felt it astoundingly come to life. Persuaded of the undeniable integrity of my companions, my accustomed, uncritical acceptance of Newtonian laws evaporated with every successive and seemingly intelligent "response" of the table to greetings voiced to unseen and seemingly highly differentiated personalities.

Varying from a creaking shudder within the wood—uncannily akin to a mere nod of the head—the movements of the undeniably inorganic and homely object ranged back and forwards through rapid swayings to violent motions of agitation.

As the sitters returned to their chairs and the medium, seated on a sofa, went into trance, the impression persisted that proceedings were being watched by an unseen assembly. I began to glimpse what mystics mean when they talk of "grace descending".

The next shock was the transformation of human personality. What had happened to the caustic-tongued, cigar-smoking, wisecracking journalist to whom I was daily professionally accustomed? Freud has long familiarised us with the dynamics of the subconscious in his analyses of psychoses and the tell-tale creative activity of our dream life.

They were all inadequate to explain what I now saw and heard in the next eighty minutes. Like customs officers, over the fast-paced years of interminable news gathering, the journalist acquires an instinct for the nuances of personality expressed in speech and gesture. This was another personality speaking through the body of the man I knew well in daily life. But it was not the man himself; it was *not* his style.

To each of us, that "Through-the-Looking-Glass" Friday evening, the message of Silver Birch was personal in context but universal in application. I need only add that his eloquence won from three of his recipients—this hard-bitten writer included—the orator's finest feminine tribute, tears, not of sorrow, but of acceptance. Such a confession will only enhance the prejudice of the sceptic. For him summer lightning has not struck out of a cloudless sky. But the Greeks knew a thing or two. I can now understand why an empire rocked to its foundations when the stupefied Croesus received a seemingly trite message from the Delphic oracle.

In accordance with the time-honoured custom of the circle I was invited by Silver Birch to ask him any question which troubled me. I told him, "I still find it very difficult to accept the problem of the suffering that seems unavoidable in this world and turns many, myself included, against God."

He replied: "Yes, but it does not turn God against them. How else would you have it? Would you expect to achieve victory without difficulty, to receive prizes without earning them."

To my comment, "I get mixed up between justice and mercy", the guide gently responded: "There *is* justice and there *is* mercy. Justice is done, if not on earth, then in our world. No one mocks the Great Spirit, because the eternal law takes cognisance of every happening. The law is perfect in operation. Love, divine, infinite, has conceived the vast plan. As there is infinite love, there must be mercy, for mercy, compassion, tolerance, justice, charity, love, these are the attributes of divinity.

"Suffering there must be. How is the spirit to come into its own, by lotus eating? Because it is not easy it is worth doing. If it were easy it would not be worth doing. It is easy when you have learned that; it was not easy before you learned it. You come again and we will take the world to bits, and we will put it together again. We will learn something from one another. Do not ever despair."

When the full story of the Hannen Swaffer home circle is eventually revealed, it will present many psychic riddles for the attention of science which—and there are increasingly encouraging signs to make us hopeful—may emerge from its present perilous crossroads less aggressively materialistic and more humbly alive to the grandeur of the cosmic horizons which beckon questing, bewildered, suffering mankind.

Meanwhile, in presenting to readers old and new this further selection of Silver Birch teachings, which are contained in the pages that follow, may I express the modest hope that no single one of you will close its pages without some solace or food for fruitful reflection in your own pilgrimage along the roadway of life.

Chapter Two

WHO ARE YOU?

Who are you? Do you know? You know just that facet that is expressed through your body, but that is only the pin point as distinct from the larger life which is beyond it.

When you say you would like to find out which is you and which is not you, you have to begin by discovering which is you altogether. Do you think that you have in this earthly life expressed anything but a tiny segment of your whole self? And do you think that the consciousness that is registered now is anything but a tiny fraction of the greater, complete consciousness that is you?

How are you to decide then which is your thought, your imagination, and which is the impression, the guidance which comes from your larger self or from higher realms that are using you?

You must get the proper perspective. You must realise that you are spiritual beings expressing yourselves through physical bodies and that the spirit is the supreme part of you. The spirit is the higher, the body is the lower. The spirit is the master, the body is the servant. The spirit is king, the body is the subject. The spirit is that part of you which is divine.

It is the self-same spirit which has created, devised and fashioned the whole universe. You have in embryo, in miniature, in microcosm, all the vast powers that belong to what you call God. If you would allow this innate divine strength to rise to the surface, to dominate your lives, you would banish every care, anxiety and worry, because you would know that there is nothing that could happen in your world over which you could not triumph. That is what you have to learn. It is not easy.

Give attention to your body as the house in which you live. But it is only the house, it is not you. Being the house, it must be kept in good condition, in good repair, so that the tenant can be amply looked after. But always remember it is only the house; it is not the tenant.

That same power which fashioned the universe is the power which is responsible for life. Life is not physical or material, life is spirit, and spirit is life. Wherever there is life there is spirit and wherever there is spirit there is life.

The power, which is you, is the power which is life and you have a kinship with the Great Spirit that enables you to participate in all the infinite processes of creation. You can call it up any time you so desire from the well of your own being—the tremendous power of the spirit that is resident within you, that is capable of giving you a dynamic, a vitality, and of sustaining you.

You have a task to perform. You will imbibe this knowledge and you will use it to help others. You will develop the gifts of the spirit yourself and when you have done so you will become a little lighthouse that sheds the beams of truth to weary souls still in the darkness. When you do that you will fulfil the purpose of your own existence.

There is a plan into which we all fit and that will operate with the consent of your free will. There is a saying in the East that when the pupil is ready the master appears. When you are spiritually ready the door will open. You will not have to ask. The door will open so wide that you will walk through it and the task will begin.

We can never promise that your life will be free from problems, perplexity, or even pain. We *can* promise that within yourself you will find the means to overcome all handicaps and disabilities. As you strive to express the highest, the deepest, the greatest within yourself, so you will attract to your aid those beings from our world who love you, who desire to help you, and through you help others.

Alas, there are too many who live encompassed by swirling mists of darkness, whose shoulders groan under the weight of their load and who know not where to turn, sick in body, mind and soul. These are the ones we must always try to help.

We would be failing in our purpose if we were to declare that the task of spiritual attainment is easy and that those who, in any measure, would attempt to spread light where there is darkness will meet with an easy task. It could never be so. The whole of history is against it, for truth and error have been engaged in a dreadful warfare that will not cease until infinite perfection can be achieved and that, in the very nature of the case, is unattainable. It is a long and difficult and toilsome struggle in which we are engaged.

You do not realise the prejudice, opposition, hostility, antagonism, misrepresentation, superstition and deliberate attack that will have to be faced. I do not say these things to daunt you, but to place any quest in its proper setting. I know how difficult it is.

I have had to overcome, with all the power at my command, almost insuperable obstacles to reach your world, and I am not alone in this. I am one of those who elected to return because it was seen that the calamities which man would bring on himself were of so awesome a character that unless the power of the spirit could effect its bridgeheads everywhere, man would destroy himself physically and the world in which he lives.

Wonderful though man measures his material achievements, spiritually he is still very puny. Oh that the achievements of the spirit could match the achievements of matter, that progress could be made in fields of the mind and spirit that are comparable with the advance that has been made in certain fields of material endeavour!

Because man is not spiritually led he is in danger of blowing himself up with forces that he is not entitled to have at his command. All our efforts are directed, wherever channels can be found, towards the single purpose of ensuring that the spiritual truths upon which the whole of life are founded should be the basis by which man everywhere builds his life.

All jealousies and bickerings, all strife and fratricide, all war and chaos, all envy, greed and malice can be driven from the earth. Compassion, kindness, gentleness, amity and co-operation can be the principles by which men rule everywhere because of the recognition of their common spiritual nature. There is a bright side. It is not a picture of unrelieved gloom, because amid such obstacles and difficulties any step forward is great progress. If you can help only one soul to be comforted when all seems drear, dark and dismal, then it has all been worth while. And you can help far more than one.

The prizes of the spirit are not easy to be won, otherwise they would not be worth winning. If the victor makes no effort, what is his victory? If you can scale peaks without labour, what have you attained? It is the very essence of the case that spiritual attainment must be a lonely, solitary path that gets more and more isolated the farther you reach because you have to leave familiar landmarks behind.

Emphasising that wherever an effort is made by any human being on earth, at least an equal, and usually a greater effort is put forth from the Other Side, Silver Birch stressed:

It is always true that any sincere request for spiritual help can never fail. You open yourself to this aid the moment you make this magnetic link with the world of spirit. It is very hard sometimes to find language that will convey the actuality of spiritual happenings because language, which is material, is not equal to the spiritual, which is immaterial. Words, at the best, are poor symbols to interpret a much greater reality.

When you accept this knowledge it means your soul is ready; it has come into its own. So many people are unconscious of their higher nature, which is the reality and the mainspring of their existence. They do not understand that the reason they exist is because they are spiritual beings expressing themselves through material bodies.

Even though they believe they have a soul or a spirit, they think of themselves in terms of a body with a spirit, whereas they are spirits with bodies. The real you is the spirit—the soul, the divine, the eternal.

The body is fashioned to serve its purpose. It has a temporary existence in this form. When it has done its task, it crumbles away. But the spirit that incarnates at birth, that is important. The fact that you can receive this knowledge means that the divine has awakened within you. You have burst the bonds. The seed has begun to flower. It has forced its way up from the darkness into the light. And it will grow in beauty and richness as you allow it to do so.

Then you begin to exercise true harmony of being which is the fundamental purpose of life on earth. Those who go through your life without allowing the spiritual nature to have its complete and proper exercise are just as handicapped as the physically blind, deaf and dumb.

Your spiritual nature has come into its own. The divine has been awakened. It is an index that points to the fact that you have reached that stage in your development when you are ready to obtain from life, not that which exists only on the surface, but all the richness that belongs only to the spirit. The riches of the spirit are far greater, far more beautiful, far more lustrous than all the gems of your world. They will endure long after the others have tarnished and rusted and decayed.

Once the soul comes into its own it realises its powers. These are part of the mightiest forces in the universe. You begin to make a channel through which help, guidance, inspiration, sustenance and wisdom can reach you from our world. This not only enables the ones who love you and who are tied by blood to come close, but others, who are in no way physically related. They have a spiritual relationship which is even more important. These draw closer and seek to bring their power to bear and help you in your lives.

As this power obtains lodgment and builds itself up, so you become the possessor of that which the world can never give or take away, a rock based on confidence, calmness, resolution. Then you know beyond all doubt that there is nothing in the whole world that can disturb the *real* you, and that you are at one with the power which fashioned the whole of life.

Men and women devote all their efforts to gain baubles and possessions far beyond what they need and sacrifice the eternal realities, which are the greatest assets the human being can have. Wherever you can, drop the seed. If you meet with rebuff, take no notice. Do not argue, do not attempt to become missionaries. You cannot force the seed to grow on barren soil. In the fullness of time some of these seeds will begin to take root. Those who have scoffed and ridiculed will come to you for help because they need it.

The tie that binds us together is the tie of divinity. It encircles us all and holds us in an embrace of divine love. Nothing can happen throughout the universe to weaken that affectionate embrace as long as we are true and loyal to that which has been revealed to us.

The Great Spirit will not fail us. We must not fail the Great Spirit. The whole of life pursues its course following ordained paths. The earth rotates on its axis, the tides ebb and flow, the stars and planets wheel across the sky following their charted course, the seasons come and go as part of the eternal cycle. The seeds grow and bloom and die, only to bloom again. Birds of diverse hues sing their cheerful notes, trees nod in the breeze, everywhere life obeys the law of which it is a part.

We cannot put ourselves outside that divine ambit; we are part of it. Let us remember, wherever we may be, that the cloak of infinite love is wrapped around us, the divine arms enfold us and we are always in the presence of that power that made us part of itself.

Chapter Three

SERVING YOUR APPRENTICESHIP

The soul knows before it incarnates what it has to do. You do not start your physical existence as a spirit without any awareness of itself. The spirit chooses the vehicle of its incarnation because it knows that that combination of circumstances will provide the best opportunities for the necessary unfoldment it has to undergo. Once it incarnates into matter, the denseness prevents the awareness, which is embedded deep down, from reaching your consciousness.

The great difficulty of people who live in your world is that they look at life, through no fault of their own, from the wrong perspective. They see life only in earthly and material terms. Life is not only earthly and material. It is spiritual, it is eternal. You cannot judge eternity by its physical span. If you do, your judgment is incomplete. It does not take cognisance of all the factors of compensation that are available to every child of the Great Spirit.

There is a plan, but it is not so rigid that those who participate in it are marionettes. You do not just dance to a string. You are imbued with part of the divine spirit. You have the chance of sharing in the process of infinite creation. Thus, you have personal responsibility and a measure of free will, but not so great that you can counteract the operation of any natural laws. Within their scope you have the power to choose. Your supreme destiny is fixed, but it is for you to unfold your latent divinity with the blue-print that you have.

You may not even be aware of the blue-print, but the soul, because it is divine, is restless, surging, striving to express itself. Sometimes it takes an experience like mourning, sorrow, suffering or illness to awaken you out of your torpor and the soul comes into its own. If the Great Spirit did not wish you to have the privilege of sharing in creation, and by so doing expressing your latent divinity, there would be no point in your being born. That is the balance that you must strike, whether you so expand your character that you choose to develop the latent gifts that you have in service that enables them to burgeon.

A dual process is at work. The bombardment is not only from without but from within. Locked within your soul is an energy greater than any known in the physical world because it is part of the Great Spirit. Without it there could be no life, for life is spirit. All matter is but the shadow, the husk of the reality which is spirit. The extent to which you are susceptible to these dual forces depends upon your awareness.

Spirit is life, life is spirit. There is no life apart from spirit, Matter is a husk, a shell, a shadow cast by the reality which is spirit. Matter of itself has no existence. You live, breathe, move, think, judge, reflect, sum up, decide, weigh, ponder, consider, think, because you are spirit. Spirit animates your frame. When spirit departs the body crumbles into the dust from which it was originally evolved. Those who worship the things of matter are bowing to false idols. There is no reality in them. Their existence is but temporary.

Spirit endures because it is the primal stuff of which all being and existence are composed. The life force expressed in human form is a variation of that expressed in bird, animal, fish, tree, flower, fruit and vegetable. Wherever there is any manifestation of life that is spirit at work.

There are degrees of awareness, degrees of consciousness, because spirit has an infinite number of manifestations. No limits can be set to infinity. You call God the power behind life, I call it the Great Spirit, because it is the apex, the origin, the summit of all spirit. All these manifestations, whatever form they may take, are expressions of the divine power which is their originator.

I regret that the path of those who serve is not easy. I did not make the laws, I only know how they operate. It cannot be that those who are to perform the greatest service should escape from the difficulties and the problems that touch the very depths of their souls, and stir into activity all those hidden powers which must be brought to the surface if the instrument is to be used.

The coin of service has its obverse side. The server must be able to serve because his own soul has been touched to the uttermost. It is only by plumbing the depths of the soul that the gifts of the spirit which that individual possesses can attain the bloom of their maturity. Sometimes I wish it were otherwise, that those who are destined to tread this path of attainment and sacrifice could live metaphorically in a bed of roses. But even the most beautiful rose has its thorns.

These are part of the truths of the spirit and I cannot change them. It would be false of me to say something which I know is not true. But the infinite spirit is perfect justice in operation. Perfect justice is something that the imperfectly operating mind of man on earth and, indeed in many spheres in our world, cannot comprehend. There is compensation and there is retribution. The scales are perfectly adjusted. No soul loses through sacrifice and no soul gains through selfishness. The index of an evolved soul, and of its attainment, is the degree to which it has lived in the Garden of Gethsemane and has thus been able to achieve its Mount of Transfiguration. This is the law of divine love in action.

There is all manner of service, some in the glare of the lights, other in the quietness of the sanctuary. What is important is that the service is given. It is important that an awareness of spiritual realities should be given to those who are ready to receive them. In a world filled with dismay and dread, when millions are fearful of what the morrow will bring, it is important that there should be an understanding of what life truly is, not its surface, but its reality.

It is important for man to know that he is an infinite soul, that his earthly pilgrimage is a small but necessary part of an eternal life. He should live that life, not in the darkness of ignorance, but in the sunlight of knowledge, not with shoulders bowed, but with head erect, not with fear, but with glorious, radiant serenity.

You are not building for the day. It is not the temporary result, the quick, brief victory. It is part of an eternal plan, an infinite campaign on which you are engaged. You cannot measure the results of what is achieved. Today, throughout many countries, what seemed formidable walls are crumbling, vested interests are being shaken, monopolies are breaking down, superstition is receding, ignorance is being driven back by the slowly advancing forces of spiritual truth.

Your fears are needless and groundless. You are in very capable hands. You are the recipient of a power which has sustained you through all the years, and without it you would have left the earth a long time ago. Fear is the greatest corrosive influence on all the things of the spirit. Fear and anxiety are the two enemies on which we constantly have to wage war because they impede the channels by which the power of the spirit can produce results.

If you always lived in the light, then the light would be of little value to you. It is because you live for many years in the darkness that the light comes with such a revelation. You must go through your apprenticeship in this world before you can qualify for ours. Those who attempt to cut short their service find they do not enjoy what our world has to offer them, not for a long time.

The plan of life is very simple. You come from spirit, incarnating into matter to obtain the experiences you need to enable you to come to our world equipped for the tasks and the joys that await you. The equipment is obtained in your world. That is where you learn the lessons that prepare you for the life after school. If you do not learn the lessons, then you are not educated, not ready for what comes next. That is true in your world and it is so in our world, too.

The wind is always tempered to the shorn lamb. The accounts in the ledger of the Great Spirit are balanced with perfect exactitude, with compensation and retribution, precisely designed to fit every action. This is another way of saying that effect follows cause inexorably. Whatever the suffering so exactly is the compensation which is the result of that suffering. Whatever the lesson, so precisely is the knowledge gained from that lesson. You cannot have one without the other. How else can you gain knowledge without learning the lesson? And then having gained the knowledge, you have the responsibility of what knowledge brings. He who sins in ignorance is not so great an offender as he who sins with knowledge, for he knows what he is doing.

You are imperfect beings with latent perfection striving to express itself. The war between matter and spirit constantly raging in your lives means that you must sin, as it is called, or make mistakes, as I prefer to call them. If you did not make mistakes you would be perfect, and nobody is in your world or in mine. That is why the Great Spirit puts you in a world of matter so that out of the interplay between action and reaction of material and spiritual forces the innate divinity learns to find expression.

It is through shadow and darkness that you come into the light. It is through storm that you come into sunshine. It is through difficulty that you come to attain. It is through conflict that you reach peace. Life can only be achieved through comparisons. Were your paths one even monotone, there would be no unfoldment. The development comes through the clash of varying circumstances which mould and mature the latent spirit. That is the whole plan ot existence.

Sometimes, to those who ponder, it seems that life is harder for some than for others. Some are freed from pain, aches, cares and strife, while others seem to live in the shadows, hardly ever seeing the light. But that is not the whole of the picture. Even if it were it would not take cognisance of eternal factors which are yet to make themselves known. I have lived much longer than you have and as a result have become a little more familiar with the working of the law to which I always pay my tribute, for I have never known it to fail.

I have never met a soul in my world to whom injustice has been done, who could say, "Now that I have seen both sides of my account, they do not balance." The Great Spirit does not make mistakes. If the Great Spirit could make mistakes the universe could not continue for another day. Long before you came into this world it was in existence and long after you have departed from it, it will still go on. Millions of years ago the sun, a great orb of light and heat and warmth, without which earthly life is impossible, shed its rays when there were no living souls in your world. The sun continued to radiate all that energy when apparently there were no human beings to receive it. Today you burn coal and release all the sun's imprisoned energy placed there millions of years ago. What a lesson in patience.

Do not harbour impatience or resentment. These defeat their own ends. The power that can reveal itself to you requires serene conditions. There is a framework, a pattern, and only within that framework and pattern can natural law operate. The Great Spirit cannot operate outside His own laws. If you want guidance and help you must provide the conditions by which guidance and help come to you. You must use the experience to build your own soul which is the only eternal possession you have. You must have confidence that the power which gave you life can sustain you, because you are a part of it and it resides within your own being. And if you provide the right conditions, that divine power resident within your own nature, has as part of its heritage the armoury of the spirit to give you all the weapons you require for every battle in life. But impatience and resentment, these are obstacles to the full, free, flowing of divine power.

You must relax, be receptive, calm, passive, quiescent, tranquil, serene, confident. You must know within that all will be well and in that spirit everything you require that is essential for your needs will come. You will not receive any credit for the easy things of life, only for the difficult ones. The Great Spirit cannot fail, you can fail the Great Spirit. Confronted with difficulty, muster the divine reserve and have perfect trust that the way is shown, and if you have perfect trust, the way must be shown. This is what I have taught for many years because it is true. Those who are able to apply this truth know that it does work. Matter is the servant of spirit; spirit is not the servant of matter. You live and breathe and move, not because of your physical body. Without the spirit that could not exist. Indeed, when spirit withdraws, the body crumbles.

Soul-mastery is not easy. If it were easy it would not be worth the having. There are no short cuts to supremacy. There is no royal road. Each soul must climb and toil for himself. But it is a great spiritual adventure full of exhilaration as you climb the peaks.

Chapter Four

PROBLEM OF SUFFERING

I would be untrue to my mission if I could offer any who come within the orbit of these truths an easy comfortable life. It is not our purpose to show you how to avoid life's problems. It is our purpose to show you how to face up to them, to conquer them and to emerge all the stronger for them.

The treasures of the spirit are far superior to any earthly riches. These are eternal possessions which, once acquired, can never be lost. Strive to acquire them. No soul has to carry a burden that is beyond its strength. No soul faces difficulties that are incapable of solution. Carrying the burden and tackling the difficulties are signposts on the road of the soul's attainment.

It is not easy, but the rich prizes of the spirit are not easily attained. If they were, they would not be worth the having. The truth is, uncomfortable though it may be, and hard to accept while you are in the throes of difficulty and doubt, for doubt comes even to those with experience, that those times are best for you.

We, who love you, often have to stand back and watch you fight your battle. We hope and pray that you will do so in that spirit which will enable you to learn the lesson and equip the soul. You cannot have knowledge without the responsibility that it brings. When you get the proper perspective you will not regret any of your sorrows. It is not when the sun is shining and all is calm and peaceful that life's lessons are learned. It is sometimes in the darkness, in the storm, that the soul comes into its own and begins to express the greatness of which the individual is too often unaware.

The whole of your earthly life is one long challenge and test. You are the centre of a battlefield in which all the forces of your being wage constant war. You have within you all the elements of strength and weakness, the remnants of the animal ancestry which are part of your physical evolution, and the divine potentialities that are the concomitants of your birth as a spark of the Great Spirit.

The whole of earthly life is a conflict as to which gains the ascendancy. That is why you come into this world. You are not created perfect, except in miniature. Being part of the Great Spirit, you have latent perfection within your soul. But all else is a struggle for development, unfoldment, attainment, as each aspect of being manifests.

Always there is free will, not wholly free, but governed by circumstances which determine your choice, according to character and temperament, as to which way you will go when you arrive, again and again, at the crossroads of your own destiny.

Each individual has the opportunities for unfolding the latent divinity with which he begins his earthly pilgrimage. He determines which way he goes, whether he lives in the light, or the darkness, whether he serves or is selfish. This is the constant struggle of human existence in your world. It explains all actions and reactions, determines the growth of the soul and its unfoldment, and whether you come to our world, when the time is ready, prepared or unprepared, fit or unfit, mature or immature, according to the way you have lived. It is simple but complex.

The more talents you have, the more gifts you possess, the greater is the responsibility. The soul knows before it incarnates what it should do with the gifts that accompany its entry into your world. He who has talents and does not use them pays a greater price than he who has none. It cannot be any other way. Grief is the great stepping stone to knowledge. Grief is one of the most profound means by which the soul comes into its own. Grief, especially when it touches the fibre of your being, enables the soul to be awakened. The soul sometimes is so embedded within the body that it requires a tremendous power to bring it out.

Grief, sorrow, sickness and suffering are part of the means by which the children of earth are taught the greatest lessons. If truth were to be found with ease, it would not be appreciated. It is because truth comes in the hour of greatest sorrow or suffering that value is placed upon it by the one who is ready to receive it. Trite though it may sound, you cannot obtain truth until you are spiritually ready.

No soul is awakened until it is spiritually ready. No soul is helped until it is spiritually ready. It is the soul's development which decides when the time is ripe for knowledge to make its entrance. It is determined by the soul and its evolution. It is natural that you should look at the universe, at life, at yourselves, through the eyes of matter and attempt to weigh, consider, assess and judge all happenings from their physical standpoint. But that is only a very insignificant part of a large story.

The greatness of the soul is discovered only when it conquers difficulty. Discouragement is good for the soul. You must learn to allow the latent greatness of the soul to express itself. That is why you are living in a world of matter. Discouragement is not the end. It is the beginning. There is a power within you that is greater than anything that has yet been expressed. The Great Spirit is not found when life is easy. The Great Spirit is found only through struggle and difficulty. The pure gold has to be crushed before its richness and beauty can be made known. The gold of the spirit cannot emerge until it has been purified and refined through sorrow and hardship. There is no other way. If some tell you that there is, I do not know it.

Your world is the world where mistakes are made. In correcting them your spirit grows. It is indeed a boon that those who are called upon to face trial and difficulty, obstacle and handicap, are, in the end, better equipped than those whose life is too often a bed of roses. The power of the spirit does not express itself when all goes well, when the sun is shining and there is not a thought to disturb the soul. The soul comes into its own when it has to meet challenge and difficulty, when it can call upon the inner, divine armoury and allow the weapons of the spirit to come into the great battle of existence that is part of the overall plan.

Do not complain about difficulty. Difficulty is good for the soul. You may not like it at the time that it comes, but you will look back and thank the Great Spirit for the opportunities that were given through difficulties to enable the gold within to be excavated. If every soul that incarnates found life an easy pattern to follow there would be no development, no unfoldment, no character, no attainment. It is a hard lesson, but the things worth attaining are those which are the most difficult. The prizes of the spirit are not come by with ease.

The Great Spirit is constantly at work, never absent, always familiar with every aspect of being. The Great Spirit's laws continue to operate, in sunshine and in storm. You cannot judge the Great Spirit. You cannot judge the universe. You cannot judge the world. You cannot judge yourselves. Material yardsticks are all too infinitesimal for that purpose. Naturally when you look at your world through the eyes of matter you see inequality, injustice, wrong-doing, the triumph of might, the despair of virtue. All that is only a very partial and false assessment.

It may be that for a time justice does not come into its own, because in a material world you cannot always have redress. But when the story is finished, the scales are always rightly balanced until not even a hair's breadth separates them. You are not the best judges of what is spiritually best for you. Sometimes the worst answer to your prayer would be to give you that for which you asked.

You must try to judge, and it is very difficult for you, every situation, not from the material standpoint, but from the spiritual standpoint. Sometimes what seems disaster to you is victory to us. Sometimes what seems triumph to you is disaster to us. If you ask for guidance you will receive it, not necessarily in the way in which you want it to come but in the way that is best for your soul at that moment of its evolution. The divine power cannot fail you, but do not attempt to measure eternity with the yardstick of earthly life.

There are certain infallible indexes of spiritual verities. Two of them I will enunciate. No harm can come to any soul whose honest motive is to do the best. Every soul who desires to serve will find the opportunity provided. Do not be impatient. It took millions of years for conscious life to be made manifest in your world. It took millions of years for that life in human form to reach its present organised form. It took many years for you and others to be aware of spiritual realities. Let the power which guides the universe, let the power which proved it is capable of guiding you, fulfil its purpose. Trust implicitly in that power which cannot fail, for if it could the universe would cease to exist.

The simple truth is that unless you had problems to resolve, battles to fight, difficulties to master, the latent divinity of the spirit could never attain a maturity of expression. It is easy for me to say it, I do not have to go through your difficulties, but I have been through them. I have lived much longer than any of you because I can count existence in terms not of hundreds but thousands of years. In the course of that long experience, I have come to regard with increasing awe, wonder and admiration the exquisite perfection of the natural laws that regulate the whole of the universe.

Nothing is left to chance. There are no accidents. All is regulated by unchanging, inflexible, omnipotent law. I know that when the soul has awakened and comes into its own and is aware of itself, the way will be shown. I have perfect confidence in the infinite power that created the whole universal system. There is none in your world who can produce any power that approaches by a fraction the power of life which enables them to continue from day to day. I know of no country or nation which can produce systems of law that will compare in any way with the natural laws that rule all life.

Why then should there be any fear or lack of trust in that divine power which has been directing the universe for all time? You must put yourself in tune with it. You must cast out all thoughts of fear and anxiety. You must learn to have inner tranquillity and serenity, complete confidence, so that through you the maximum of divine power can flow to fulfil its purpose. When you are in harmony with the law of love and wisdom it works itself out. The wind bloweth where it listeth. Love finds its own. Love, divine love, of which human love is but one expression, is the fulfilling of the law.

The simple truth is that those who have knowledge of spiritual realities should face each day without a trace of fear and know beyond a shadow of a doubt that the Great Spirit within gives them automatically the possession of such an armoury that they can fight any battle which they are privileged to encounter. They must triumph, for the power of the spirit is mightier than any material force.

Fear is the worst enemy of mankind. Fear is corrosive, Fear saps, drains, vanquishes reason, overwhelms, keeps away the very power that would enable you to conquer every difficulty. Fear disturbs, prevents harmony, stops attunement, causes wavering and doubt. Banish fear. Those who have knowledge should be tranquil, radiant, serene, confident, impossible to be disturbed.

If what I say were not true, matter would be superior to spirit, darkness would be greater than light, ignorance would triumph over knowledge. The power of the spirit, which is the power of God, is supreme throughout the whole universe. The spirit is not only all-powerful, it is all-wisdom, it is all love. Behind all life's manifestations is the divine wisdom.

It is in the fire that the steel is forged. It is in the hour of difficulty that the spirit calls upon its latent, infinite divinity and allows it to find expression. These are invaluable sign-posts on the path of your life. Just as the darkest hour precedes the dawn, so the light of the spirit must shine. All that is required is that you should discharge your duty faithfully and well, and rest your confidence in the power which has revealed its loving beneficence towards you.

The soul that has knowledge must realise that frustration and setback are equally parts of the plan, as are advance and progress. The negative and positive, action and reaction, are opposite and equal, these are the two sides of the coin. You cannot have the one without the other. There is a law that sets in motion the means by which you can advance. There is a law responsible for frustrations and setbacks. All is part and parcel of the same complex, intricate pattern, designed to allow the human spirit to find its fullest expression. You cannot have all-knowledge. Where your knowledge cannot take you, you must have faith, not blind, foolish, credulous faith, but faith founded on knowledge.

Knowledge is the unshakable base, the enduring foundation. Knowledge, which has revealed the eternal truths of the spirit, in turn should produce complete, unwavering, unrelenting, undisturbed confidence in the power of the spirit which is the life-force itself. The fears in your world, the wavering doubts, these disturb the atmosphere. We work through tranquillity, through certainty. When you disturb the atmosphere with fear, doubt, anxiety, apprehension, you block the path by which the power of the spirit can reach you.

It is easy to thank the Great Spirit when the sun is shining, when all is peaceful and there is plenty of money in your bank. The time to thank the Great Spirit is when you are in the darkness, given the chance to let latent strength lead you to the light. That is the time to thank the Great Spirit, for that is when your lessons are learned, your spirit grows, your mind expands and you begin to reach the stature that should be yours. Nail your colours to the spiritual mast.

What your world does not understand is that spiritual truths cannot be received until the soul is ready. The seed cannot grow until the soil is fertile. It is there, divinely implanted, but you must provide the appropriate conditions, the sun, the water, the air that are necessary for the seed to burst its bonds, to grow and then to flower in all its wondrous beauty.

There is only one way that the soul can find itself and come into its own. It is through the path of travail, sorrow, suffering, what seems to you darkness. Your soul will not be touched while life bubbles along for you and there is naught to draw your attention to the underlying, eternal, spiritual realities. And so it is that the plan of the Great Spirit is shown, that knowledge makes a lodgment within sorrowful preparation. Once knowledge makes a lodgment within you and you begin to be at one with the power that fashioned you and in harmony with the laws of the Great Spirit, then you are expressing the gifts of the spirit, its richness, its beauty, its lustre, its nobility, its dignity, its grandeur, these priceless gems that are part of your birthright.

Once you have acquired this knowledge, you cannot lose it. Your soul has made its magnetic link with the world of spirit and you are open to receive what can be, when you are ready, a flood of power and wisdom, of inspiration, truth and beauty. To each one of you there is given that amount of free will which, as you evolve, you learn to exercise.

The higher you evolve in the spiritual scale, the greater can you exercise your free will. You are your own limitation, but, because you are part of the Great Spirit, you can conquer all the difficulties and obstacles in your world. Spirit is superior to matter. Spirit reigns supreme. It is the essence out of which all life is made, for spirit is life and life is spirit.

Chapter Five

THE FOG OF MATTER

Sometimes, people like yourselves, who are immersed in the day-to-day work of your world, burdened with its cares, concerned with its problems, occasionally dissatisfied because of the uncongenial conditions in which you are compelled to labour and the too often unsympathetic attitude of those who should be colleagues, are apt to forget the great shining ideal which first presented itself when just as on the road to Damascus a great light shone.

The pristine beauty of the vision is apt to lose some of its radiance and it is not always possible to recapture the glory in which it first manifested. And yet the tasks on which we are engaged, each in our several ways, fulfilling duties which we have undertaken, sometimes at our own request, have an importance we cannot always estimate. You who live in a world of matter, encased, obscured and imprisoned by a physical body, are unable to have that clear perspective as to the relationship of spirit, mind and body. The cares of your world press upon you, the requirements of your physical nature have to be met, you have to concern yourself with the necessity of obtaining the coin of your world. In this constant task, you are sometimes apt to get out of focus and are unable to feel the nearness and presence of those whose joy it is to sustain and uphold you.

It is part of my willing task to remind you on such occasions as this that, whether you are conscious or not, you are surrounded by love which guides you unerringly in its divine purpose. It is not always possible, when you desire it, to show you the light of the spirit, or to reveal the beauties of the larger life which are around and about you, but they are there just the same.

A fog may obscure the vision, but it is only a fog which can be, and is, pierced by the radiance of spiritual light which emanates from our world. Just as that light and that power guided you into this field of service, having often prepared you by years of constant watchfulness for the task, so it continues this mission, ensuring that your feet do not stray and that, if occasionally you miss the track, you are brought back to it so that you may continue to walk on one of the many pathways that lead to the Great Spirit.

The truth is that you are very richly blessed, for you are the possessors of a knowledge so priceless that all earthly riches are poor when compared with it. I say this in the hope that it helps you to understand your lives, as we see them. We do not see the earthly world through physical sight but from a realm where values are different and standards are not those of yours. Our judgment is, we think, the one that is more real.

You are so engrossed in matter that it chains you down to its low vibrations. You awaken in the morning and before your consciousness is completely functioning a thousand and one material cares begin to engulf you. Before long you are so immersed in these problems, some large, some small, some real, some imaginary, but all of them transient, that you forget the power of the spirit is exercising its beneficent effect on you. You almost shut it out of your thinking and build a kind of wall that makes it more difficult for it to penetrate.

It is such a familiar story with all the instruments of the

spirit. The pattern is repeated time and time again, the enthusiasm, the despair, the Garden of Gethsemane, the Mount of Transfiguration, the constant see-saw of the human soul struggling to find itself, express itself and enable the latent divinity to rise to the surface. This is nothing new. It is the history of every instrument, every seer, prophet, visionary, of every inspired man and woman. There is an ebb and flow, like the movement of the tides. But, as I tell so many instruments of the spirit, there is a pattern in their lives. If they look back, they can always see the guiding finger that has pointed the way.

The divine plan exists even when you cannot see it. It works itself out ceaselessly to fulfil its allotted task. There are, in all human lives, times when you will fail to see the pattern and will ask questions, why? when? how? what? whither? which, of course, you are entitled to do. All I can say is the plan is there. In a universe which gives evidence of regulation by the greatest of all powers, it is impossible to attribute results to chance, coincidence, or haphazard happenings.

Before you came into this world, like everybody else, your soul knew what it would undertake. The difficulties, the obstacles, the setbacks are part of the process by which the soul comes into its own. The richest prizes are the hardest to attain. If they were easy, they would not be worth attaining. That which is easily achieved is quickly forgotten. That which is most difficult to attain, the unfoldment of the Great Spirit within you, is the hardest of all.

Life moves through comparison. Light and dark are servants of the Great Spirit. If there were no light and dark, then dark and light would be the same. If there were no morning and night, then night and morning would be the same. If there were no love and hatred, then hatred and love would be the same. It is the comparison that enables you to understand the difference, but they are only opposite ends of the one pole. You cannot go through earthly life with a monotone. You must have light and dark; you must have warmth and cold; you must have happiness and sorrow; you must have the variety of experiences to enable the soul to come into its own.

Perfection is never achieved because it requires infinity to attain it. I hope I do not speak in riddles. In the constant process of seeking perfection each step forward brings another step in view. Like knowledge, the more you acquire the more you realise there is to be acquired. There is no finality to knowledge; there is no finality to wisdom, to truth, to understanding, to spiritual attainment, because these are all part of the Great Spirit which is infinite.

There is nothing in your world to fear. Fear is the great enemy; fear saps the vitality; fear prevents the spirit from finding expression. Drive out fear. Perfect love casteth out fear, and love rules the universe; there is no place for fear, which belongs to the darkness of ignorance. With knowledge you should live in the sunlight of spiritual understanding. He who worries indicates that he is actuated by fear. You have nothing to fear but fear itself. Fear belongs to the darkness, not to the light. A soul that has complete, unswerving confidence in the power of which it is an integral part does not worry.

The power that enables you to breathe is the power that fashioned the universe; the power that gave a place to every star and planet; the power that gave the sun its inexhaustible radiance (no matter what your scientists say); the power that controls every ebb and flow of the tides; the power that enables every seed to fulfil its purpose and grow into a multitude of different forms of sentient life. That power throughout all time has never failed. Has the tide ever ceased to ebb and flow? Has the world ever ceased to revolve on its axis? Has any natural law ever failed to operate?

The world of matter is only part of your life. It is not your eternal home. It is because, unconsciously, so many of you think that you are living in the world of matter all the time that your difficulties arise. You and I are in the same universe. We are not in watertight compartments. The universe is one in which every aspect blends and harmonises and merges into the other. By dying you will merely express another aspect of your consciousness and cease to register in the physical body.

I know the problems that confront you, but those with knowledge must learn to strike a balance and not give to matter the preponderance of their attention. The power of the spirit must dominate. If you have the right perspective, if your focus is true, if your daily outlook is balanced, you give to the requirements of matter what is their due and no more. Then you allow the spirit to work its will, to permeate and flood you and fill you with that dynamic which can transmute the whole of daily life, until you reach the stage where you know that nothing material can really touch you.

You cannot judge eternity by your daily happenings. You tend to make judgments based upon the coloration of your mind, by the circumstances which surround you. It is because, being encased in matter, and faced with the daily problems that throng about you from the moment consciousness wakes in the morning until it sleeps at night, that you are apt to forget what has been achieved.

Turn back the pages of the past for your comparison and that will show how the finger of the spirit unerringly has pointed the way all the time. Those who are blessed with knowledge should be able to live from day to day with their heads upturned, never with their heads downcast. Knowledge teaches them that the power of the spirit cannot fail. Men and women in your world can fail the Great Spirit, but the Great Spirit cannot fail them. What you require for your sustenance is always available to you, if you put yourself in harmony with that law which provides infinite possibilities. These are the spiritual truths which all must remember.

He who has seen into the world of spirit has caught a glimpse of that larger life. Knowing something of the cosmic pattern he cannot be irresponsible, for such a person is more conscious of his duties and responsibilities to the world in which he lives. He does not neglect them, nor does he allow himself to be overwhelmed and to give an undue preponderance to the things of matter. All security and sustenance are to be found in the spirit. The whole world of matter and your physical bodies exist solely because they are expressions of spirit.

As this truth begins to dominate your life, so there comes that inner tranquillity and serenity that accompany the knowledge and enable you to give a true assessment of everything which is part of your daily life. I am not suggesting for a single moment that any individual in your world should falter in duty, or neglect a single responsibility. What I am saying is that the common fault, even with those who have knowledge, is to forget the underlying important spiritual truths on which the whole is founded. Once you have seen with the eyes of the spirit and learned the foundation on which all life rests, then you can banish fear which is the great enemy. Knowledge is the armour which will always protect you; fear corrodes and rusts.

If the Great Spirit allowed me to transfer one gift, what I would love to do is to give the power to see to those I love, because I have such pity for you in this dark world in which you live. You have no idea of the radiance which is around you. You cannot see this beauteous universe in which you dwell. This fog of matter clouds everything. It is as if there is a thick bank of cloud obscuring the rays of the sun all the time. If you could see the radiance around you, you would know that there is no real trouble that could penetrate it.

We are subject to laws and conditions. We can do only that which lies within our power according to what prevails at the time. Whether visible or invisible, audible or inaudible, tangible or intangible, the power is there to fulfil its function of guiding, maintaining and sustaining. I have always said to those who serve that, no matter how dark the days may seem, they will come through, for the power of the spirit is the power of life itself. Life cannot exist without spirit. Life, its whole essence, vitality, potential, dynamic, all these are due to its being spirit, precisely the same in essence, though differing in degree, as the Infinite Creator of all things.

It is hard to appreciate all this when you live in a world of matter with all its illusions, but it is my duty to tell you that reality is in the invisible and must not be confused with what you see purely in glimpses. It is only when you withdraw into the inner planes that the vision is clear. I am not very concerned with labels, or troubled with organisations, except if they exist to be instruments for spirit power. My task is to try to be a guide, a teacher, to offer a little wisdom, based on garnered experience, to those who are ready and prepared to receive it. Another aspect is, in conjunction with colleagues, to help the flow of spirit power so that the divine will can be more easily seen and more people harmonise their lives with it.

To me, what is important is the instrument. It is only through human instruments that the power of the spirit can operate. Thus, the problem remains a constant one, to find more and more instruments through whom spirit power can be registered. The power is infinite; the number of instruments is limited. There cannot be too many because there will always be power available for however many through whom it can be expressed. But just as it is said that the wind is tempered to the shorn lamb, so the power of the spirit can be absorbed only by the capacity of its instruments. They cannot absorb more than they are capable of receiving.

The law of evolution is seen at work in the individual, as well as in the race, or in the nation, or even in your world. So you are bound to get the ebb and flow of the tide in the various assemblies that are concerned with the flow of spirit power. What you must not confuse are the assemblies, the buildings, the organisations, with the flow of spirit power. You cannot monopolise the power, you cannot command it to flow this way or that way. What you can do, as individual instruments, is to offer service, making yourselves the purest possible channels and thus the greatest amount of power that can be absorbed will come through you.

Having said that, I would add that there is more spirit power operating in your world today than there ever has been, and through countless channels. It is not even restricted to mediums. It operates through many who are unaware that they are instruments. The self-same power is utilised in other movements.

The plan does not change. You have to change and fit into the plan. If you place yourself in harmony with that divine power and allow it to guide you from day to day, then you will fulfil the purpose of your being. The power of the spirit does not work according to earthly standards; it cannot be hastened or accelerated and forced into this channel and that. The wind bloweth where it listeth.

The stars wheel in their courses, the tides ebb and flow, the seasons follow one another, all as an integral part of this majestic, stupendous, sublime scheme. You cannot change it now, but as part of it you can allow it to work through you and thus help to share in the infinite processes of an eternal creation. You, by virtue of your heritage, are spiritual beings, part of the Great Spirit. The Great Spirit is you and you are the Great Spirit. In lesser degree, in embryo, in miniature, you are the microcosm and the macrocosm is the Great Spirit. Thus there is for you access to all the infinity of the Great Spirit, as by increasing spiritual attainment, growth, progress and evolution, you make yourself receptive to it.

Gradually, as light triumphs over darkness, knowledge triumphs over ignorance. The law is growth, change, evolution, progress, unfoldment, development. Know that always there is a tide, an ebb and a flow, a circle, a cycle, a spiral, all part of the evolutionary process, simple on the surface, but complex and profound beneath. You will get the surge and the regression. You will get, in times of material prosperity, an ignoring of spiritual realities, and equally you will get in times of difficulty a demand for spiritual realities. It is all part of the warp and woof of the plan behind the whole of life.

If you ever become satisfied with the progress you are making, then you are making no progress. If you are discontented, searching, seeking for new fields to conquer, then you are evolving. It is said in your world that nature abhors a vacuum. You cannot stand still. You must go forward or backward.

The spirit is restless because it is part of the creative power of all life, always seeking new outlets, and thus it cannot feel content. If it cannot find an expression through mediumship, it will thrust its way through the artist, the philosopher, even the scientist. Concern yourself with what you can do to increase your spiritual awareness and the service you can render to others less fortunate than yourself. Labels do not count. The arguments in your world over the labels of religion, politics, art or economics are of no importance. The service that the soul renders determines its evolution.

The Creator is not mocked. The law operates, effect follows cause, reaping what has been sown. There are no miracles, no dispensations. The natural law will always operate with unfailing regularity, immutable, unchanging, inflexible, mathematical in all its exactitude of precision, irrespective of man's systems. You will have victories and defeats always, but the soul that is aware should not let itself be troubled by either. There will come a time when the scales have fallen from your eyes and you will be able to judge by eternal standards.

I would not attempt to minimise your problems and difficulties. I am too familiar with them. But I would be failing in my duty if I neglected to point to the eternal values which you cannot, at present, assess. Throughout all history there have been times when some beat their breasts with lamentations. They thought all had failed, that they would be swallowed up in the darkness and no more heard of the things for which they stood. But the universe has continued to function and so it will.

All I can do is to reiterate for you the truths that will stand for all time. It is for you to adopt them and mould your lives on them. It is not easy, but if it were easy it would not be worth the doing. Nothing in spiritual exploration is easy. The path of the spirit is the hardest of all to follow. Sainthood, mysticism, mastery, these cannot be accomplished with ease. It is a long, slow, arduous, tortuous path which has to be followed, with constant sacrifices. Renunciation is the law.

If it were possible for the highest prizes of the spirit to be gained without struggle, this would be making a mockery of eternal wisdom. Put that way you must accept it. I have never said that the Great Spirit is not the author of light and dark, of good and evil. The Great Spirit, being the Great Spirit, must be the author of everything. You cannot exclude some aspects of universal activity and say that something, some body, some power is responsible for those. To me the whole of the universe is in a state of polarity. You cannot have anything without its opposite.

You only know there is darkness because you have seen light. You only know there is light because you have seen darkness. You only know there is good because you have seen evil. You only know there is evil because you have seen good. The power that causes the light and the dark, the good and the evil, is the same. The way that the power is expressed is not the fault of the Great Spirit primarily but in the free will of the individual. That is his choice, that is his development.

Your world was never created perfect. Individuals were never created perfect, but only with latent perfection. The latent perfection is their spiritual heritage, its unfoldment is their responsibility. It is the exercise of their free will. You decide whether you shall be good or evil, selfish or unselfish, merciful or cruel. Do not forget that your union with the divine is indissoluble. It provides you with a means of indrawing strength and power and helpfulness, but you must learn to retire into the quietness of your own soul so as to obtain the closest possible attunement.

We are all bound by ties of mutual helpfulness and service, contributing something important to one another's natures. Let us rejoice in what has been revealed to us. Let us use it as a foundation on which to build our confidence in the power that gave us birth and that continues to nurture us. Let us strive always to be its instruments, through whom this power can flow to help others less fortunate. And let us at all times remember that we are in the presence of the Great Spirit, that the plenitude of that power is available to us if we but reach out to assimilate all that we are capable of absorbing. It is an infinite power that belongs to an infinite spirit with infinite potentialities.

Chapter Six

PROBLEMS OF COMMUNICATION

Seldom, if ever, is a communicator able to impart the totality of his communication. It is possible only in exceptional circumstances. It is not as if you are making a communication on one surface of being like a telephone. Even that goes wrong many times; when lines are crossed, the machinery gets out of order and sometimes will not work at all. If you have these difficulties in communication on one surface of being, realise how much more difficult it is when you have two entirely different states of being.

You have to make vocal what begins as an image, a thought or an idea in the mind of the communicator. With a trance medium control is never one hundred per cent effective. The instrument is a human being. Control varies according to the guide's success, partial success, or failure in blending with the medium's aura. The guide takes possession through the subconscious mind and all the bodily processes that are controlled by it. Whilst doing so, he must transmit, if possible, the original image, thought, picture or idea that comes from the communicator. The medium can be tired, ill, out of sorts, bad-tempered, hungry, had too much to eat, to drink, to smoke, a thousand and one things; all can affect the closeness with which guide and instrument should blend.

There may be subconscious ideas in the mind of the medium, strong, dominant, which keep on thrusting their tentacles because they are trying to find expression. Often the only way to get rid of them is to express them and make them null. That explains sometimes why you get the medium's subconscious ideas expressed by a guide. Sometimes the guide cannot help himself and is carried away by the onrush, the force of the subconscious promptings. Fog is bad, so is humidity. A cold, clear, crisp, electrical atmosphere is the best.

It is not easy. It requires much effort to return to your world. That is why the only ones prepared to make the efforts are those who love you. Love is the impelling motive for comforting, guiding, helping those to whom it is naturally and willingly bound. As long as people die, and they love those who are left on earth, they will willingly break through every barrier and overcome every obstacle to reach the one they love. That provides part of the impetus behind the whole of communication from our world.

Be tolerant. Do not blame the medium. Do not necessarily blame the guide. We do our best with the material at our disposal. To accomplish in trance, what is being accomplished now, requires a stepping-down process, the use of a transformer. That involves a sacrifice of the true individuality to a large extent, as you can appreciate. When you have to make it material you go one stage further. You have to materialise the spirit and to have almost a complete reversal of vibration from the subtle, quick and delicate to the slow, heavy and ponderous. That, of course, also means another sacrifice of the whole individuality.

Then, again, there are subtle deviations of ectoplasm, according to the mental and spiritual qualities of the human instrument. Not all ectoplasm is the same because its basic foundation is extracted from the medium. The grosser the instrument, the less refined, the less mentally and spiritually evolved is the ectoplasm. Where you have a refined soul, mentally and spiritually, those qualities are reflected in the ectoplasm.

It does not follow that every person who desires to communicate in our world is able to do so, or, given an opportunity, is able to transmit the fullness of the message. It depends on the individual. A dominant, forceful individual will break through all the barriers. A shy, diffident, retiring individual will not want to make the effort.

Then there are all the processes involved in transmitting the thought, picture or symbol—we do not speak words in our world—through the medium's guides, or even direct to the medium. If it is done by means of clairvoyance, all this is a very intricate process. Do not think that because you hear me talk with facility through this instrument that it is easy. Even I have to use what I call a multitude of "threads" to maintain my hold on this instrument. At any given moment, any one of these "threads" may be severed and away goes some of my power.

We have many problems to elucidate in the understanding of communication. Do not ever let it be said that it is always easy. When you have the right conditions, it can be very easy. But there are so many factors that can interfere, and sometimes because of these factors we are blamed. It requires the operation of very delicate, subtle conditions, even for one who is experienced to act as a go-between. There are so many factors that can go awry.

You realise that in this process of transformation, this stepping down, much of the beauty, lustre and radiance must be lost. But when spirit communicates with spirit direct, when mind communicates with mind and soul with soul, when there is inspiration or imagination, it merely means that the mind is being enriched with impressions from beyond. The more you worry about it the worse it becomes, because to be successful in its transmission the essential condition is a quietude, a passivity, a confidence based on the certainty that attunement is taking place. Once you set up wavering doubts, these by their very nature clog the lines of communication.

I do not wish to suggest that every thought which reaches your mind has its origin in our world. Obviously that would not be true, but it is true to say that you must not be quick to dismiss as imagination so much that is the result of deliberate effort to enrich your mind and soul.

Always remember that it is not like a communication in your world where there is only one plane, one level of consciousness involved. You have to reduce spirit to matter, two entirely different forms of expression, and in that process of stepping-down many things can go wrong. We have a long way to go in perfecting the means. In our world there is constant experimentation, research and investigation in every field of communication, in the mental, physical and in healing. Always there is activity in trying to achieve a better result.

That is why you see the improvement made as years continue. That is the purpose behind gatherings such as this, because it is only through the constant providing of conditions that we can develop your powers and bring to bear a large measure of the power at our command. They have to be harmonised, so that the results can become effective in your world. The important thing is that the lines have been laid, the channels are open, and we can transmit. There was a time when there were hardly any lines, and hardly any channels.

Why people in your world prefer the darkness of ignorance to the light of truth is something I do not understand. We are always concerned with those who can reach and help other people. Every new channel is one more means of spreading knowledge, of spreading spiritual power and working towards the amelioration and betterment of the whole human race. This is a great truth which is part of an infinite truth. There is a serious purpose which underlies the whole of our work. I am only one of many ambassadors, part of a vast plan created in a world beyond yours, directed to help those who are ready to be helped.

We must keep on touching souls, awakening slumbering souls, getting them to realise the greatness that could be theirs. We offer them gifts of the spirit that bring with them the full lustre of their own dignity and grandeur. If obstinate man refuses this, he is turning his back on the greatest gifts offered by the greatest power in the universe.

We have nothing to offer but the truth, and it is the truth that will set men free. Why this should incur enmity, displeasure, hostility, opposition and misrepresentation, I do not know. Maybe they are mistaken. Their judgment has become warped and they are incapable of realising that there can be truth outside themselves. Sometimes I think they must think that it is very wrong of the Great Spirit to reveal His wisdom outside their organisation. But as it is said, "The ways of God are not the ways of man." Perhaps it is good it is not so.

In the case of the churches you have a great difficulty. You have men who earnestly believe that theirs is the truth and they are defending what is to them something very dear. They do not realise that their system has been built on something which originally was divine in origin but has been overlaid through the centuries by what was devised from the mind of man. They cannot isolate the original from the wrapping. They worship the wrapping as being divine. If they have become fossilised mentally and spiritually, nothing can reach them. The Great Spirit has ordered it so that through some mental or spiritual upheaval you are given the opportunity of finding truth, but it does not always happen. If through trouble, sorrow, sickness or sadness their souls are touched, then the experience has been worth while.

The whole purpose of the return from our world to yours is to draw attention to spiritual realities. It is as simple as that. We could easily be unconcerned with your world and its activities. There is no compulsion to associate ourselves with you, and you have no means of forcing our attention. Our efforts are voluntary because we love you, with the whole of humanity, and desire to help you. It could even be argued that perhaps our love, like a good many forms of love, is a little selfish because we have seen so many come to our world unfitted human wreckages, not ready and poorly equipped. It becomes so much easier if they learned the lessons in the place where they were intended to learn them, the schoolhouse of earth.

The whole purpose is to draw attention to spiritual realities, to show that every being starts the physical course with a spiritual heritage conferred by the act of birth. The life force is the divine spark, spiritual in nature, which is intended to grow equally with the physical body. The majority of mankind concerns itself only with physical growth. Some of it is concerned with mental growth, and a few concerned with spiritual growth. The only enduring reality is spirit. If we succeed by a variety of means in making man aware of his spiritual nature which is his reality, it transforms the whole of his life. He sees its purpose, is conscious of his origin, becomes aware of his destiny and should live his life in the implications of the knowledge which he has received. That very simply is the plan behind all our activities.

When it is applied to daily life, then you will drive away all fear, worry, discord, hatred, disease, selfishness and pride, and there will truly be peace based upon a genuine spiritual brotherhood. Increasing awareness of these eternal truths makes your souls and your spiritual bodies receptive to the powers from our world. That is the magnetic link between earth and ourselves.

In order to reach your world, we must have the means of doing it. We must have the channels through which this power can flow. Part of your psychic and spiritual unfoldment consists in becoming more and more receptive to our influences. As your soul natures blend with your spirit co-operators, so they can transmit through you that power which can help in times of crisis, difficulty and danger. This power is hard to define because it is impalpable and intangible from the material standpoint, but it is none the less real. It is part of the force of life, it is part of the Great Spirit, it is in essence the same as the power which gives consciousness and being to every facet of activity in the universe. It is the same power that enables the seed to grow and to blossom, and another seed to fruit, the tree to grow and a soul to unfold itself.

It has an infinite number of possible manifestations. It can revive, resuscitate, reinvigorate, recharge and revitalise. It can inspire, it can heal and, when the conditions are suitable, it can produce physical results in your world. When you retire into your own sanctuary for the purpose of giving healing to others, as a corollary you are also unfolding your own channel for receiving spirit power. The two go together. Often when people sit in circles for development and nothing apparently is happening, a great work is being done in strengthening and unifying the links between matter and spirit, for the transmission of spirit power is a highly intricate and delicate process.

If people were highly developed and their lives were more spiritual than material, instead of, as at present, more material and less spiritual, then the task would be easier because the common nexus between us is spirit. Alas, with the vast majority of individuals, the spirit is so deeply embedded, so embryonic, so latent, that it is with the utmost difficulty that it can be reached at all. Some are so engrossed in matter that the spirit within them is but a tiny flicker, so small that it produces practically no light. But it is there. When they are ready, after they have been in the crucible of suffering, then they too can be awakened, then they too can be aware, then they too can understand spiritual realities, themselves and the Great Spirit, the link between them and everyone else and all creatures, and realise the fundamental bond of unity that is part of the natural law.

When you open the door of your soul to one form of knowledge, you must not close it, but must allow the processes of unfoldment to continue. You will not attain perfection in your world, but you can strive to improve your mental and your spiritual outlook.

There lies always the larger task of reaching the many whose lot is not so rich as ours in mind or spirit, to bind up broken hearts to show how the sick can be healed, to emphasise those eternal spiritual truths which are the only foundations for societies to endure, to drive out and banish all the fog and mist, the error and superstition, the vested interests that are the obstacles to the full flowing of spirit power that can illumine and beautify and dignify the world in which you live.

It is not an easy task for people who are invisible, so far as you are concerned, and who are impalpable, so far as worldly sense is concerned, to make their impact on a world of matter. As long as you maintain a good heart, a willing spirit, a receptive mind and undimmed faith, then this channel is open and you automatically are the better for it in all respects, spiritually, mentally and materially. What so many people do not realise is that when they do not get the answers to the things that they want, it is because they themselves do not provide the channel by which the help can come. We have no hands apart from yours. In order for spirit to make its mark upon matter, it must have some nexus that is responsive to spirit and can express itself in matter. It is so simple when you realise it. All I would urge is to go on and know that the power which is sustaining and supporting you is the divine power and it will not fail in its task.

If you succeed in enabling one soul in darkness to find the light, one troubled, wearied individual to gain strength, if you comfort one mourner, if you heal one sick person, if you prevent exploitation of and cruelty even to one animal, then indeed your earthly life has been well worth living. Never weary in the fight for the things that matter. This is the greatest of all fights, the eternal war against materialism, selfishness, these cancers that are festering in your world today and lead so many on to foolish paths where they perish in the darkness without a realisation of the purpose for which they were born into the world.

No effort for good is lost, no attempt to help is futile. Never be weary in your well-doing, never be disappointed if you do not see the results. Just go on and know that every attempt to serve automatically calls to your aid beings from our world who will lend their aid to your labour. You never work alone. Always you are surrounded by the host of the shining ones whose arms will support you no matter what circumstances arise. Place your complete faith in and rely on the power which cannot fail you. There is no security in your world at all. The only security is in the unseen, the invisible, in the eternal realities which cannot be measured by any apparatus in your world.

Your security is the strength of the spirit, the majestic power which is the means by which the Great Spirit expresses itself everywhere. When all else has changed its form, either by being reduced to ashes or by crumbling into dust, the realities of the spirit will still stand, unchanging, immutable, as the unshakable base on which to build. I know it is very hard for you, living in a world of matter in which all is measured by your physical senses, to appreciate the nature of reality. It escapes you all the time. But if I can convey, in however inadequate a form, the fact that spirit is the enduring substance of all eternity, and that nothing else matters, and if I can encourage you to build on truth and not on shifting sands, then at least I am helping to fulfil my mission.

Chapter Seven

THE JOY OF SERVICE

There is no joy and no service that can match helping others. In a world so full of darkness, where millions have lost their way, where there are countless numbers troubled and perplexed, with sorrow in their hearts, who awake each morning in fear and apprehension of what the day brings, if you can help one soul to find some serenity and to realise that he is not neglected, or lonely, or forgotten, but surrounded by arms of infinite love, that is a great work. It is more important than anything else.

The whole purpose of earthly life is to awaken dormant, slumbering souls to the reality of their existence. Your world is full of living sleepwalkers who go through the day's activities in a dream. They are not awake, and they are dead to all reality. If you can touch one of these souls and kindle the divine ember so that gradually it is fanned into a living flame, there is no service comparable to that. When all is said and done there is no higher privilege, no higher religion, than service to the Great Spirit through serving all His creatures, human, animal, or whatever form they take.

Fortunate are we that we can be used as ambassadors of the Great Spirit who has chosen us for these tasks. These cannot in themselves make us happy when we contemplate the misery of everything that need not be. If we can help, if we can drive out ignorance, if we can banish superstition, if we can replace cruelty with kindness and exploitation with mercy, if we can show a better way, a way of co-operation and amity, then gradually, as it spreads, there will be a true peace amongst all creation because peace is indivisible. The power of the spirit is at work, and it is here to stay. No fiat of the Church, no edict of doctors will prevent its labours of mercy. This power can succeed where all others fail.

There is no greater service and no greater fulfilment than to watch the power of the spirit performing its beneficent labours and bringing relief and health, alleviation and comfort, guidance and sustenance to souls who do not know where to turn but who have been led to you. This is a work greater than that done by many churches, chapels, synagogues and temples which are filled with dry, arid theology, but where the power of the spirit is absent.

The sick, the suffering, the tortured in mind, body and spirit, the hopeless, the helpless, the weary, the perplexed, these do not want words, which too often the ministers no longer believe themselves. They do not want to hear the stereotyped phrases repeated in parrot fashion that have no meaning to the speaker or hearer. What they want is a demonstration that spiritual truth is a reality. When you offer yourselves up in service and allow your divine gifts to be utilised, spirit power flows through you, with its wondrous healing touch, to smooth away pain, to restore harmony, to free aching and locked limbs and to make the individual aware of himself as he really is.

In the work in which we are all engaged there are often setbacks. We have to deal with human beings, alas too often full of frailty and weakness, pride and vanity, prejudice and obstinacy. Too few will place service before self, principle above person. If you look back, you will see clearly and unmistakably how the finger of the spirit has pointed the way and divine signposts have shown where you are to go. That power which has proved itself without a doubt and question is competent to guide you in all the labours and days that lie ahead.

It is always more blessed to give than to receive. Blessed are they who have not seen and who have not heard but who continue to labour. You have the warmth, radiance, affection and love of enlightened beings whose only aim is to help those less fortunate than yourselves.

Every soul knows before it incarnates into earth what it is that it will undertake. It is a free choice made by the larger self because it knows that its earthly journey is precisely the one needed to fulfil and obtain the necessary qualifications for the development of the larger self. You know the life that you are going to live. The hardships are chosen because to endure them, and to overcome them, will bring into play those latent qualities of the self which require development to add their quota to the real, the higher, the true self.

There is, in one sense, no need to say, "This is a great pity", or to wonder about the inequalities and injustices of earthly life. Ours is the world where the balance is struck. Yours is the world where the preparation is made. When I say that the soul knows, I do not mean it knows every detail, but it knows that path that is to be trod. It is all a question of time and interplay of varying forces as to when the soul comes into its own and is aware of itself. Sometimes that does not even happen, and so the soul comes back, again and again, until it attains the qualifications that are necessary for its fragment to pass on to the larger self, to the whole.

It is very difficult for you to pass judgments on yourselves, your progress, your unfoldment, because you have not the means by which you can measure. You cannot see with the eyes of the spirit. All your judgments are faulty because you are looking through the eyes of matter the whole time. You cannot measure the effect on the soul, which is all-important. What happens to the body is important only because of its effect on the soul. If what happened to the body did not affect the soul then it would not matter. You cannot force the hand of the spirit. You cannot compel the Great Spirit to move in your human way. The divine plan unfolds itself unceasingly. The wise individual, wise because he has knowledge, learns to co-operate with infinite love and wisdom.

The acquisition of this spiritual knowledge is not to be obtained with ease. It is accompanied inevitably by hardship, physical, mental or spiritual. Sometimes it is a combination of two out of three of these factors, and sometimes a combination of all three. The road to spiritual attainment is a thorny, difficult one. As you move along it, the familiar landmarks and signposts are left behind. Loneliness, increasing loneliness, is the lot of the pilgrim who treads it.

But just as there is retribution, condign in its nature for all the selfish and unkind acts of earthly life, so equally is there compensation for those who essay the path of the spirit; for increasing awareness brings with it an inner life, an inner radiance, an inner glow, an inner confidence. It brings an increasing awareness of the eternal foundation on which all life rests, and an increasing awareness also of the mantle of divine protection that is thrown around your shoulders. I have never said that it could be easy. The greatest prizes, the richest prizes that are worthy of possession, these are the most difficult to earn. And they must be earned by every individual for himself.

I have lived many, many years in your world and in mine (as you count time in your sphere of three dimensions). I have grown to marvel more and more at the efficacy of the natural law which comprises the whole cosmic system, and takes cognisance of every happening. I know that the spread of knowledge, the awakening of the soul, and the appreciation of spiritual realities—all these every individual must accomplish for himself, entering his own Garden of Gethsemane before he can achieve his Mount of Transfiguration.

There are no short cuts, no vicarious means by which the spirit can come into its own. There is no ready-made formula, no need, no ritual, no ceremony, no doctrine, no book, however sacred, that can provide the easy way to the adept, the pupil or the initiate. Self-realisation must be earned through struggle and toil, for only by these means does the soul come into its own. I deliberately say all this, not because I desire to read a lecture or to preach a sermon. It is an attempt to convey some of the truth which I have learned.

I also know, and can affirm without fear of contradiction, that those who desire to serve, those who are actuated by the motive of helping the less fortunate than themselves, the sick, the bereaved, the seemingly hopeless, the ones who feel their burden is too heavy, who are weary and perplexed and think there is nothing left to live for, in short, all those who seek to serve humanity in whatever sphere, they will not fall and stumble without the means being made available for them to raise themselves up.

Sometimes it may seem that the clock is about to chime midnight. But before the last chime is heard, the power of the spirit, if you allow it, will achieve its divine will. Those who have knowledge should weather every storm, resting their confidence on an inner tranquillity, an unshakable serenity, an implacable determination born of the knowledge of the certainty of spiritual realities which are the foundation of all life.

You attract by your service, not only those related to you by ties of blood, your own kith and kin, whose passing brought you into this knowledge, but those angels whom the Great Spirit has given to be in charge of you, and who have watched you from the moment of your entrance into the world of matter and who have truly acted as guides the whole way. You cannot measure the work you have done. But it is stamped indelibly on your own soul and on the souls of those you have helped to come into their own. Be rightly proud of the labour that has been done. Thank the Great Spirit that opportunities are given you to perform this service. It is the richest work that you can do.

Do not worry about the foolish, needless jealousies, the petty spites. You have a protective armour to ensure that they cannot really touch you unless you allow them to do so. The strength of the spirit is your refuge. The love of the spirit is your sanctuary. The wisdom of the spirit is your haven. Seek them whenever the need arises. Earthly minds may fail you, but never will the power of the spirit neglect you. Realise always that guidance continues to function even when you cannot see it, and that the arms of love always encircle you.

If I can say one word to encourage you, to cheer, to enthuse you, then I rejoice. It is instruments we need. I am not concerned with buildings, churches, temples, institutions. They have their place, but the power of the spirit flows not through masonry but through human instruments who are important to us as links in the mighty chain. One honest servant of the spirit who allows himself to be an instrument is more important than all the buildings. Just go on. Do your best and continue to serve, serve, serve wherever you can. Seek no plaudits of your world. Know that you are fulfilling the purpose for which you were born, so that when the time comes you leave with no regrets for unfinished labours.

Let us rejoice at the opportunities given to each one of us to serve the greatest power in the universe by bringing enlightenment to some of His children. Let us rejoice that we are fulfilling the purpose for which we were created. There is no religion higher than service. To heal the sick, to comfort the mourner, to guide the perplexed, to give strength to the weary and direction to those who have lost their way, those are the most important tasks of all.

Rejoice, therefore, that you have been brought within the orbit of service, with the means, ability, gifts and the power to express the love of the Great Spirit. Rejoice that you wear some of the divine emblems. Know that always in your labour you attract to yourselves the power which will help you always to continue to serve. Never forget that the supreme purpose of life is the unfoldment of the spirit. Pay attention to the requirements of your eternal nature. Thus you have a true perspective and focus on life and know that you are immortal souls, expressing yourselves through mortal clay, and that strength will come as you allow the divine to express itself through you. These are the important principles to be borne in mind. They are hard to remember when you are engaged in daily conflicts and matter seems so powerful and spirit so weak. But spirit is master and matter is servant. Spirit is king and matter is subject. Spirit is God and you are part of God.

This is the great joy of service, to be able to know from day to day that you are fulfilling the purpose of your being, that the power of the spirit is freely flowing through you, touching souls for the first time and enabling them to be awakened, to be helped, to be made whole and to be given a fresh opportunity to enjoy all that life has to offer. This is truly a great work. Wherever it can be done, in any corner of your world, it does not matter, as long as the light is brought to a soul and spiritual truth begins to permeate. That is important. All that has gone before is a preparation and nothing has been lost. The soul always has to be prepared for its task and sometimes it means going through the valley before you can get to the top. I have often said that in order to rise to the top one must have been to the bottom.

Your earthly standards of valuation are not the same as ours. Your world worships many things and attaches importance to them, whereas here we regard them as insignificant. All that makes people crave position, wealth, authority and power, we regard as unimportant. When the body dies they all die with it. But the service that has been rendered cannot die because in doing it you increase your own spiritual growth. The service that is given out of love and affection and devotion all help to increase the character and so make an eternal hall-mark on the soul.

Earthly plaudits are unimportant; popularity can be easily won and lost; it does not matter. But if you know within your heart and soul that you have truly rendered the greatest service you can give, then indeed you have developed your powers to their zenith and you have done your best. You have that power to co-operate with enlightened beings in our world who can use you to demonstrate eternal realities of the spirit. That is a great and important task. You help to spread truth, knowledge, wisdom and understanding so that those who can be reached begin to know the purpose of their being, the reason for their being placed in your world and what they have to achieve before they leave it.

The test is the application of knowledge to life. It does not end with an enriching of the individual's own mind. It is not an acquisition for personal satisfaction. It is a responsibility to try to share it with others, for in the act of sharing you gain all the time. That is the spiritual law. You cannot convince people of spiritual truth. They can only convince themselves. You cannot convert people; they can only convert themselves. Spiritual power must work its own will, and not until the soul is receptive can the individual accept the truth. We are not missionaries who desire to proselytise. We are preachers of the true gospel, the good news about spiritual realities. But only those who are ready to receive the news will understand what we have to say. Those who do not understand are not spiritually ready.

They are like those of whom it was said in other times that it was like casting pearls before swine—that is not intended in any odious comparison. We cannot change individuals; they must change themselves. We are not our brothers' keepers. We are responsible for our actions, not those performed by others. It is the work of a lifetime in your world to ensure that your actions, your thoughts, your words, your aspirations and desires are in harmony with the knowledge that is revealed to you.

That is all that you can do. You cannot live the lives of others, even though you love them, because it is contrary to the law. If those who have knowledge behave in a way that contradicts the knowledge, they will pay a greater price than those who transgress through ignorance, for knowledge always brings responsibility. The soul that is aware of truth commits a greater offence than when a similar action is performed by a soul that is unaware. That must be so.

Every time you touch a soul you are helping to fulfil the divine purpose. That is the most important work you can do. You enable the soul to come into its own, and it is more than anyone else can do. Co-operation is the law. We would never attempt to dictate, to supplant your reason, to rid you of your free will. Our function is to live up to our name to guide. Whatever effort you make, we will make a greater one to meet you and help you. Together we can labour in fields which are important because they concern the very fundamentals on which the whole of life rests.

Many, alas, mistake the shadow for the substance, the husk for the kernel. They do not know reality. They live in a kind of miasma, if living it be. Fortunate is he or she to whom the light of the spirit has been shown. What can I say to willing servants, but "Go on"? The infinite power of the spirit will always sustain you. In days that you call good or bad, never will that power leave you. It will be the strength to support you in moments of weakness.

Strive to remember who you are, what you are and why you are here. Even with all your knowledge there are times when, immersed in the day-to-day problems, you are apt to overlook the eternal realities. It is these eternal truths to which you must cling. There is nothing else in the whole of your world of matter which can provide you with a foundation on which to build your lives. Spirit, not matter, is the reality. You may not be able to see it, or touch it, or feel it.

You may not be able to experience its reality in the manner in which you obtain material sensations, but it is still the master of all. Realise that you belong to eternity. You are but pilgrims treading a temporary passage through life.

Chapter Eight

HEALING AND THE LIFE FORCE

I would like you to know of this great power which is in your midst, power which enables you not only to heal the sick but to touch the souls of those who are ready to be awakened to an understanding of the great eternal truths. This is the whole reason for healing. If you put right what is wrong with the physical body and you do not touch the spirit, then the healing has failed. But if you touch the spirit then the healing has succeeded, for you have helped to fan the divine spark which can now grow in illumination and strength.

This always is the purpose behind the work of healing. Healers were born into this world in order to help the plan of the Great Spirit, to bring realisation of eternal truths and eternal realities to so many of the children who do not know who they are, why they are born into your world, and what it is they must do before they leave it. That is the greatest work of all. If you succeed in awakening *one* soul, then your life on earth has not been in vain—one soul, and that is enough to justify your existence.

I rejoice that the work is growing and that more and more are turning their thoughts towards the power of the spirit. When those we love meet with troubles we always come to their aid as best we can. When it is sickness, then a greater force is applied to help. But you must remember that every effect has a cause. Whatever help is given from our world cannot be interposed between cause and effect. We can help, but we cannot eradicate the effect that is due to a definite cause. You are souls expressing yourselves through bodies. There are laws which control the body as there are laws which control the soul. If, as a result of the operation of the law, something happens to the body, that is cause and effect. By spirit power we can help, but we cannot eradicate the cause that is due to an operation of the law.

We cannot work miracles. We cannot alter the natural sequence. The Great Spirit is always at work, never absent from the universe which divine power has created. Nothing happens without the knowledge of the natural laws which encompass all things. The sick man who is healed, when all other avenues are closed, is the best living testimony to spirit power. He recognises that he has been brought face to face with a power greater than anything he has encountered on earth.

If his soul is touched, which it should be, and I believe there is no successful healing until that happens, then he has come into his own and he has begun to fulfil the purpose of his being. There are many people, both outside your movement and inside it, who do not understand the underlying fundamental purpose. The varying phenomena are important in the part they play, but they are only toys, designed to direct the attention. You cannot play with toys forever. You must grow from childhood to manhood. And when you grow you should not require the toys that are given to amuse children and hold their interest.

There are many forms of healing, starting from the purely magnetic, which can be physical, to the psychic, which can be non-spiritual, to the highest, which is spiritual, when, if the instrument can so attune himself and the patient is ready, healing can be achieved without any touch of any kind. You can, by the sheer magnetism of a healthy body, transfer that magnetic power and not touch our side of life. You can reach the halfway house, by which most of your absent healing is done. Then, as I have said, there is the final attainment, in which a healing can be performed without any touch at all, by the attunement between the instrument and the forces operating so that healing is instantaneous.

The divine power is within every soul. You can tap that power because you have access to the armoury of the spirit within yourself, for the Great Spirit is within you. Just as the physical body, obeying the natural law, will always attempt to heal itself, so you, as a spiritual being, if you follow the natural law, could heal yourself.

Health is wholeness of body, mind and spirit. It is the harmony of the three essential ingredients of man while he is on earth. If any ingredient is not functioning properly, then there is a lack of alignment and you have sickness, disease. The way to achieve the harmony is for each aspect of man's expression on earth to fulfil its allotted part. The power of the spirit performs its beneficent task and none can gainsay it. Those who seek to deny it, or to thwart it, always have to face the consequences.

You are witnessing the same power in miniature that is responsible for the whole of creation, for the energy residing in the ocean, in the pull of gravitation, in the movements of the planets, in the multitudinous manifestations of growth in human, animal, vegetable and in every kind of life. Healing is part of the life force. That which gave life to the body is the spirit. Matter does not possess life of itself. Matter has no consciousness apart from spirit which endows it with life. The principle that enables you to live is the same principle which flows through you in the healing to bring those wondrous results to the afflicted, the stricken and the diseased.

Thus, in a way, you share with the Great Spirit the responsibility of utilising the infinite powers of creation itself. Any who seek to tamper with this must regret it. In times of old, the great sin was against the holy ghost, the holy spirit, the power of the spirit. As you open out to receive its fullest influx, so you automatically receive the benediction that flows with it and which emanates primarily from the author of all being.

There is a great work to be done in a world that is sick, physically, mentally and spiritually. A part of our task and your task is to drive out that sickness of body, mind and spirit, to bring an understanding of love's purpose to those who are wandering in the mists of confusion, groping to find their way. That is the supreme purpose of *all* mediumship. To give a message to one whose heart is heavy with sorrow, whose eyes are filled with tears of sadness, that is good and helpful and important. To give healing to one who is racked with pain, tortured by illness, or afflicted by disease, that is merciful and very necessary.

These are the precursors; they are the means, not the end. The thing is to awaken and touch the dormant soul, so that it comes into its own. If the soul is awakened and begins to understand the purpose of its incarnation on earth, then you have fulfilled your part in the vast scheme of regenerating your world, which is the whole reason for our collaboration. That is the key that unlocks the door. It is more important that a soul shall come into its own than a body should be healed, or that a mourner shall be comforted, because that is truly fulfilling the divine purpose. You have not succeeded until that is done.

If you bend your energies to that task and realise that behind *all* aspects of mediumship and communication that is the important part, then you are fulfilling your own destiny, for that is the reason you were born into this world. Spirit power is infinite; it has no limitation, except that imposed by the instrument through which it comes. Without the instruments the power cannot be expressed. They have to broaden and deepen their capacity and concurrently develop their spiritual natures, which determines the amount of power coming through them. Then there are tremendous forces which can be unleashed through them. There are no limits. The spirit potential has no bounds. Always from our world elevated beings are at work experimenting with the instruments at their command, striving to obtain the greatest combinations of force, to produce better and quicker results. We have not reached finality in our world. We can only do the best with the material at our disposal.

The spread of knowledge of healing takes a long, long time. The whole method by which the power of the spirit works in your world is not to ensure any speedy or mass-conversion, but to allow this divine power to work its will on one person, one child, one being at a time, to achieve results and establish, as it were, a spiritual bridgehead that will be consolidated and made permanent. It must be that the power of the spirit, in all its diverse manifestations, not only in healing, but in other forms, will prove itself, its efficacy, as souls are ready to be helped, either with healing, with teaching, with demonstration. But the crucial point is they must be ready to be helped.

You break a law and you disturb the alignment of matter, mind and spirit. Spirit power in healing will work to re-stimulate the divine energy within the individual so that true alignment is once more achieved. Gradually, as more and more of these spiritual triumphs are achieved and knowledge of spiritual triumphs is broadcast and knowledge of spiritual realities is understood, there will be a twofold result; there will be less disease and it will be easier for spirit power to fulfil its purpose.

It is not part of the plan of the Great Spirit that attempts at achieving health should be made by the sacrifice of any living creature. There are alternative, natural methods by which all diseases can be arrested, helped and even cured. As long as man ignores natural methods of healing and persists in using animals, who were not placed on earth for that purpose, he will fail to promote health and well-being. True health is harmony, the correct alignment of mind, spirit and body, each functioning efficiently as three parts one whole. You do not achieve this by wreaking cruelty on animals, by taking substances from them which were never intended for human use. You will achieve health when man learns to live in harmony with the natural laws of the universe. Then he will die physically, not from disease, but from old age, because his body has served its purpose and he is ripe spiritually for the next phase of his existence.

If the body suffers, it is because neither the mind nor the spirit has found itself. When the spirit is right and the mind is right, the body is right. All that happens in the body reflects what happens to the mind and spirit. They call it psychosomatic now, but labels do not matter, it is the eternal truths that count. If the soul is sick, the body is sick; if the soul is healthy, the body must be healthy. Healing bodies, that is not important; touching souls, that is important.

If you make the body well and the soul is not touched,

you have failed, we have failed and the individual has lost his way. He has had his chance but has not taken it, for the object of his sickness is to reveal to him the purpose of life and what he must do to fulfil his being. So touching souls is all that matters. Truth is truth, it cannot be altered. This is the truth. There is the Great Spirit within every child, and the Great Spirit desires to find expression because only in doing so can you derive from life the richness which should be yours. It is as simple as that. If you don't express the spirit you are not fulfilling yourself.

This is the reason for suffering, this is the reason for sorrow, this is why it is only in the darkness that you find light. What emerges is the beginning of what should be a tremendous spiritual adventure. And that is what the Great Spirit intended earthly life should be, a tremendous, continuous spiritual adventure in which all would derive the fullness of its wisdom and grandeur, its beauty and lustre, its dignity, its nobility, its immeasurable wealth. This is what earthly life should be, but it is not. Materialism prevails, selfishness dominates, greed is at the helm, not service, not co-operation, not the desire to uplift, not the wish to help.

You can rejoice that the opportunities of service are presented on a road that opens out wider and wider. Yes, it is good to free the body from pain, to soothe the ailing mind, to touch the soul, and help the prisoner to be free. That is what matters, for once the soul finds itself and reforges that link with the divine power, then the individual begins to live. If the healer removes the blockage, the divine power can flow through the channel. The blockages are ignorance, wrong living, wrong thinking, pride, vanity, jealousy and frustration. Man must learn to live according to the natural law, in harmony with the Great Spirit, with himself and with all others who share the world with him.

Suffering is not the whole of the story, only part of it. You cannot have a world without suffering. It is a condition of evolution that there must be suffering and difficulty. You are not in a perfect world. You do not have perfect physical bodies; you have incipient perfection within the soul. The whole purpose of life is for this incipient perfection slowly to grow and to evolve closer to the source which gave it birth. Within that gigantic, cosmic scheme there is an interplay of forces which are all part of the evolutionary scheme. Life is not static. Life is a constant movement in which there is development all the time in ever-increasing circles or spirals. It is only when you realise the purpose of life that you have an inkling of how the whole scheme works.

None receives healing until the soul is ready to receive it. That is why even with the best healers there are failures. The failure is not a criticism of the healing. The soul of the patient is not ready to receive it. All is governed by natural law. There are no tricks; no healer has the power to alter, vary, change, or deflect the working of the law.

Strive to achieve the greatest possible attainment with the power of the spirit; that is all I can urge you to do. The more you can blend your souls with the souls of those who use you, the greater will be the results that you achieve. The work will go on. People are always difficult. It is not a perfect world. If you were perfect you would not be here, so you must be tolerant. If you think you are in advance, it is your responsibility to be more tolerant.

Never be weary in serving others. Service is the coin of the spirit; service is the entire currency of the Great Spirit. You have the strength you require for all your tasks, but choose that which must be done today and forget that which can be left for tomorrow. If the strength is limited, eke it out. Better to do that than to dissipate it and be compelled to rest.

It is only a body, just a machine which has its limitations. Any machine which has tasks imposed upon it beyond its limitations must break down. There is no machine in the whole of your world which is subject to so much work and with so little rest as your physical bodies. These are the precious temples of the spirit. They must be watched and guarded and husbanded.

I know that all who are engaged in service, no matter what the field, get weary and tired and depressed sometimes. It seems as if the battle cannot go on. But it can and it will, for spiritual truths and spiritual realities will prevail in the end. The greed, the selfishness, the cruelty, the harshness, the severities, the wickedness, all these must and will be extirpated, so that there can be peace on earth, not only between man and man, but between man and the rest of creation which moves forward together in concert and in unity.

It is not only man that is born to be free. The whole of creation was born to be free, none of it to be enslaved or tortured or exploited by man who was given the responsibility of dominion over them. And always the price must be paid, the law of cause and effect must come into operation. Man cannot betray the divinity which gave him birth and allows him to have any being at all.

All life is inseparable. There are no deep divisions, though there may be material differences. Life is one. Spirit is one, and spirit is the God which is within all forms of being. I only wish that the veil could be lifted from your eyes and you could see the radiant beings who co-operate with you. Every difficulty is a challenge which you must meet and overcome, thus proving that the power of the spirit is stronger than the power of matter.

Chapter Nine

LOVE IS UNDYING

Love cannot be measured; love cannot be weighed; love cannot be dissected with any scalpel or instrument: but love exists. Love is the greatest power in the universe. Love is the fulfilling of the law. The whole universe exists because of love. It is this love which guides its destiny and the destiny of every living creature throughout the whole of being. This love is the motivating power and is responsible for breaking down the barriers between the two worlds of matter and spirit. It enables those who have made the greatest journey of all to retrace their steps and to proclaim that message, old, but new, that love conquers death.

Give yourself to the power of love which has led you and tries to increase your receptivity so that you can become a greater channel. As sure as night follows day, as summer follows spring, as the seed bears its fruit, so the power of the spirit will unfold itself and each step on the ladder will bring you nearer to the fulfilment of your own being. Retire when you can for a few moments from the earthly scene with all its hustle and bustle and allow the inner spirit to manifest so that the tremendous latent, dynamic power of the divinity within yourselves finds expression.

Have no fear in your heart; banish it completely. The power that has guided your life for so many years will not desert you. It has sustained you throughout and will fulfil its task, as you must fulfil yours. The gifts with which you were endowed still have their part to play. Behind those who love you in our world there is the power of the Great Spirit itself. That power is incapable of failing.

The universe exists because of divine power that is infinite, limitless. Yet the overwhelming majority of beings in your world can register only the tiniest fraction of all that power because they do not provide the conditions to allow it to reach them. You have to learn, all of you, how to open your hearts, minds and souls to receive the fullness of the divine benediction which could be yours. To do so, you must learn to cultivate confidence, trust, faith, peace, tranquillity.

In that atmosphere you become recipients of the vast riches that infinity has to offer. That is the law. That is how it works. The power is limited to your capacity to receive and to assimilate. Increase the capacity and you will receive more. It is as simple as that. As you gradually banish sadness and sorrow, the clouds lift and the sunlight of certitude can reach you in growing measure.

It is divine love that makes the universe possible, that guides the universe and those who dwell in it. The reflection of the divine love which members of the human family feel for one another enables them not only to serve those they love, but others who are in no way tied to them by links of blood relationship. Love inspires them to serve those who are less fortunate than themselves. The love that is the apex of all life, the foundation of all life, the source of all life, filters through human beings, seeking to express itself in greater measure, so that in the fullness of time the whole universe will be encircled with the love of the Being who endowed it all.

It is easy to love those you love. There is no virtue, no

saintliness, in that. But to love those you do not love, that is the attribute of an evolved soul. To go to those who hate you, to serve those to whom you are not attracted, that is hard. It is difficult, but the ideal of the difficult must always be in front of you, to strive to achieve that which is hard, for that is the true measure of service. To be charitable to those who win your sympathy, that is not difficult. To be compassionate to those to whom you are attracted, that is not difficult. But to serve those who are your enemies, that is the hardest.

The highest is the most altruistic form, loves because it must, loves because it knows that love is the fulfilling of the divine law. To heal a child with an appealing face, that is easy, but to heal someone who is misshapen and whose very appearance induces repulsion, that is difficult, that is service. True love never seeks to be measured. It loves because it has no other means of expressing itself. The Great Spirit is infinite love and seeks nothing for itself. The higher you go in the scale, the greatest beings that you can reach, never demand, never request, never ask. They merely give.

I wish that could be said for people in your world. We are condemned by those who do not understand us, but we require nothing for ourselves. We only desire to serve those whom we can serve. May you all learn to respond to the highest planes of spirit. May you all realise that you are never alone, but always encompassed around and about by a host of those who love you, who seek to guard and guide you and to help and inspire you. And may you, as you unfold your own spirit, realise that you are being drawn closer to the greatest spirit of all, becoming more in unison with His laws.

Faith, that is faith alone, sometimes fails when the winds

of bitter experience blow. But the faith that is born of knowledge provides a foundation which is so strong that no wind of circumstance can disturb it. Blessed are those who believe and have not yet seen. But thrice blessed are they who know and, because they know, place their faith in that which is not yet revealed to them, because they know that the laws of the universe are operated by a power which is love and wisdom.

We are able to demonstrate that life is continuous because it is life and because it is spiritual. Thus every individual can be aware whilst on earth that he is a spiritual being, not a physical one, that he is a spirit with a body, not a body with a spirit. His entry into a world of matter is part of a priceless heritage. He associates with matter because he is spirit, and spirit gives animation and life to all that is material. That spirit is part of the Great Spirit, divine in essence, similar in quality, different only in degree.

As you live lives of unselfishness and altruism, with the desire to serve, so the Great Spirit that is within you finds fuller expression and you begin to fulfil the purpose of your being. It is not wrong to have a personal love. It would be better to apply it to a wider circle. It is better to have love in action than love in inaction. There is no quality that is incapable of having its highest and its lowest forms, its brightness as well as its darkness.

Very often love of a family is selfish, a love of blood ties. Often it is governed by a protective instinct and is a remnant of the animal ancestry in the evolutionary stream. But love is capable of its highest aspects when it will strive to love all without thought of self, without reward, without warmth, but because it is self-abnegation, the divine in action. Love desires to serve, to uphold, to comfort. Love is expressed in mercy, compassion, kindliness, goodness. Love is revealed in renunciation and sacrifice.

Why do you think that your loved ones who have passed to our world return to you? For the vast majority death is a reward, a liberation, a release from prison. They are entitled to all that our world has to offer them. They have said farewell to old age, infirmity and the many problems that harass the denizens of your world. Yet, despite all the tremendous obstacles that stand in the way of communication between the two states of life, they return of their own free will because they love you. Where their love is they are. Where their love is their treasure is also. They desire to serve because they love. It is for this supreme reason that no matter what hostility may be directed against us, no matter how gigantic may seem the forces which oppose us in our world, they will fail.

Rejoice at what you have received. Rejoice in what you have been able to share. Rejoice in the knowledge that love is stronger than death and that whatever stands in the way is overcome by love seeking its own. Let the love that is around and about you comfort, uphold and sustain you. It is there in a richness of measure that I cannot convey to you. I try so hard sometimes, but even with my command of your language I find it too inadequate to express thoughts which can convey the depth of love showered upon you by those who are closer than the beating of your own heart.

You have seen love in your world enable many wondrous acts to be performed, of altruism, heroism, service, self-abnegation, but you cannot measure the potency of the love that comes from an evolved spiritual being who gathers part of the life force itself to enable him to place the protective mantle around your shoulders. You cannot receive unless you are ready to receive. This is the way the spirit works. It is so simple when you understand it; qualify and you receive. The amount to be received is infinite. What restricts it is your capacity. Always in our world are those who are ready to give you more when you are ready to receive it. They cannot give you what is beyond your capacity.

Always look up, never down. The sun's radiance comes from above, not from below. The sun is but an emblem of an eternal radiance. The spiritual sun can fill you with illumination and vitality. It can stimulate the spirit within yourself. There is nothing in your world of matter that need cause you to be downcast, as long as you remember you are eternal by nature and all that happens is part of a pilgrimage. You cannot learn spirituality in a book. You cannot be taught spirituality by a teacher. You have to earn it by your own life, by your deeds. Spirituality is the burgeoning of divinity within the individual.

It is the power which holds us always in its embrace of infinite love, which seeks to guide us so that we truly fulfil our noble heritage and thus achieve our divine destiny. It is the greatest power in the universe, responsible for all manifestations of being, majestic or minute. It is the power which is conscious of our needs and strives to show us how we can attain them. It is the power which would lead us always into those paths which would make us increasingly aware of who we are, what we are and what we could be. Let us, therefore, in this knowledge rest content that it will always guide us with benevolence. Let us surrender ourselves to its loving care and know that we are in the hands of the Great Spirit of love and wisdom.

Perfect love casts out fear. Knowledge dispels fear, for fear is born of ignorance. Where there are love, trust and knowledge, there fear cannot reign. An evolved spirit cannot be afraid at any time, because he knows there is no experience that can come to him in any phase of life that he cannot master, for he is the Great Spirit. The love which has surrounded you will never fail. It is the infinite love of the Great Spirit, shedding its luminous rays through countless channels, striving to reach and uphold all those who seek to serve. This mighty power will always sustain you. In your time of weakness it will give you strength and in your time of sorrow it will give you comfort. It is the protective band welded around you, unbreakable because it is divine.

What we have to offer is the proof that love is undying, that death is powerless to separate those whom love has joined together and that death cannot act as a prisoner for a spiritual being once it has escaped the thraldom of earth. It is not until you come to our world that you understand the real meaning of love, because love, in essence, is of the spirit. Love is the quality that binds souls and minds. Love is an expression of the Great Spirit. Love is the desire to make whatever sacrifices are necessary in order to serve. Love sees no ill, no hurt, no harm. Love desires nothing for itself.

Death is a reward; death is freedom; death is liberation; death is the second birth; death holds the keys of life and opens the prison door to allow the inmate incarcerated for so long to enioy life as it could not be enjoyed in your world. Death, as you call it, cannot part those whom the willing tie of love has bound. This is only another way of saying that the Great Spirit's laws will always prevail. Love is an expression of the divine law and triumphs over all man's foolishness, ignorance, wilfulness and prejudice.

The real love is the union of two souls. The Great Spirit, with infinite wisdom, has ordained that each of the sexes is complementary to the other. And where there is the complete merging there you have the real love, for each supplies what the other lacks and the duality forms the unity. Because it is part of infinite spirit, it has an infinite number of variations, ranging from the lowest to the highest, from the magnetic and physical bodily attraction through the mental, to the spiritual which is the basis. In your world it is very rare, it is the exception not the rule for the two halves to meet. When they do, they find one another and become whole. This is the natural marriage of souls.

It is the ancient teaching of the affinities, the soul affinities, finding expression. In a process that takes millions and millions of years you can see that the meeting of two halves or affinities is not usual because they have to be born at about the same period. When they are, it is part of the divine plan. And beyond your world these two beings continue in their merging through aeons and aeons of time, not only shedding all aspects of personality, but as the individuality emerges, so the process of blending continues.

Love is stronger than blood. Love is stronger than death. Love is the permanent force because love rules the universe. Those whom the Great Spirit has joined in the bond of love cannot be separated in life or what you call death. The grave has no power to curtail love. Love is triumphant because it is part of the Great Spirit. And what belongs integrally to the Great Spirit is indestructible.

Chapter Ten

WHAT IS THE SPIRIT?

I cannot give you a complete picture of the spirit because it is infinite. All words are finite and even when assembled at their best still remain poor and clumsy substitutes for the intrinsic power I am trying to describe.

You all know that the Great Spirit is not a personal, vengeful, cruel, despotic being. As I have said many times it is the Law, and the mind behind it, the power responsible for the boundless cosmos without which life in its myriads of manifestations could not function. It is the power which is life itself, the primal substance of which all life is composed. It embraces the most minute and the most majestic.

In this dim, comparative way, we grasp stumblingly some glimpse of what we really are, the Great Spirit in microcosm, the whole universe in miniature. It is too vast a conception for any to grasp. Your purpose in incarnating is to express more of its innate divinity. The expression is a process that is never finished, for development, like the Great Spirit, is infinite. Automatically your spirit is expressed in all the virtues, in acts of goodness, kindness, sympathy, toleration, compassion, mercy, friendship, affection, love. Thus the more good you do the greater is the spirit that is being made manifest. Now let us ask how we can consciously seek to unfold some of this latent tremendous divinity.

There are many schools of thought, techniques, processes, each having a common objective. It is to still the physical nature, to quieten the brain and to encourage the emergence of the inner individual so as to obtain a greater harmony with the spiritual forces of life. In essence, all these techniques are concerned with your withdrawal from the maelstrom of matter into the silence of the spirit. It is not for me to outline any special technique. Each individual must find the way for himself.

There are certain processes of concentration designed to achieve the one object of allowing inner potency, which is seldom expressed, to take control for a while and establish its closer and more conscious contact with the hidden but very real power of life. As you achieve growing success, you find that you become the recipient of greater inspiration. The psychic side of your nature unfolds. Then the spiritual aspect develops and there comes flooding into your being the power that belongs to the higher reaches of life.

By the use of some techniques you can achieve self-healing and learn how to drive impurities and imperfections out of the physical body. You can learn also how to achieve a closer harmony between all aspects of your being. Gradually as you do so, allowing your spiritual nature to attain the superiority which is its natural state, so you grow in inner wisdom, understanding, peace, confidence, serenity and awareness of your true relationship with the everlasting power.

You have, because you are spiritual beings, all the latent power of the Great Spirit. You are the Great Spirit, the Great Spirit is you. You all contribute to the infinite power of the Great Spirit. The act of earthly birth is the incarnation of part of the Great Spirit into matter. That part contains potentially all the divinity of the Great Spirit. This is the seed that can flower with infinite possibility.

When the gift is there, it can be expressed unconsciously by impact from our world. It is obviously preferable to have conscious rather than unconscious guidance. And it is obviously preferable to have unconscious guidance than no guidance at all. You automatically attract those who can help you to help others. So you get the restless stirrings of the spirit as it desires to express its latent gift in service, until the time comes when the soul becomes aware of itself and consciously is ready to go forward to fulfil the purpose of its being.

The psychic nature is the in-between stage of matter and spirit. When you begin meditation, seeking awareness and releasing inner powers, the psychic faculties will be the first to quicken. This happens before the spiritual faculties operate. There are some who believe, wrongly in my view, that development of psychic faculties is a deterrent to development of the spiritual nature, that it is preferable to try and climb into the highest possible spiritual realm by oneself. This could be very difficult and sometimes fraught with danger.

The higher you evolve the more you realise that co-operation is part of the law. None lives to himself alone. All are mutually dependent on one another. We are all endless links in an endless chain. Why should the tyro reject the help of the expert? We come back to help you, and as you are helped, you help others. This service is the reason for our existence. You are constructed, not to live in isolation, but in willing concord with everybody else. This outlook must spread throughout your world, the realisation that all are linked, that no individuals, classes, castes, or countries can rise by themselves and leave others behind.

All must rise and fall together, not only the humans but the animals too, for all life is one and mutual interdependence runs throughout the whole infinite scheme. Besides it can be said that there are some who are selfish in their desire to reach out and achieve a kind of superiority that despises any other way. I am against the teaching that any one soul can live to himself alone. As I understand spiritual law, it is co-operation and no one can cut himself off completely from others. It is not necessarily selfish that you should want to achieve your own mastery unaided, but this is not the way that I recommend. To me service is the true coin of the spirit. I live for service, service to me is the expression of the Great Spirit. Let others who disagree go their way.

All the great exemplars have tried to show by example, through healing, through comforting, through giving strength to the weary, through service, that the soul is uplifted. You express yourself by service, that is the Great Spirit in action. I am sure that if you help one soul to dry its tears of sorrow, if you heal one sick person, if you uplift one fallen individual, if you give the hand of sympathy to your brother or sister in distress, that is the expression of the Great Spirit. All who say it is wrong to do so are wrong. It is right to help, it is wrong to refuse help. It is the motive which counts, but it is better to have service given from vanity than no service at all. If it is done for the wrong reason, then the soul of that individual who is the giver is not helped. None cheats the law, which is perfect. That is why it is said, "Charity suffereth long." Goodness is its own reward.

Any who work as instruments of spirit power are touching souls all the time, and that is the most important aspect of mediumship. To give comfort to the mourner, to heal the sick, to give a demonstration of spirit power in all its aspects, mental or physical, these are very important and no one can gainsay that. But their purpose goes beyond anything physical. Their purpose is to touch the soul of the individual so that it becomes awakened to reality. Your world is full of so many millions whose souls are still slumbering, who are dead to truth and who have yet to awaken.

The function of all mediumship is to make the individual aware of himself, so that his own soul comes to the fore, he realises that he is a spiritual being. Having become conscious of his spiritual nature, the divine seed implanted within him as part of his natural heritage should begin to grow. From that moment the individual is playing his part in helping the infinite creative power which is responsible for the whole universe.

Before any individuals can be qualified to be instruments of the spirit they must undergo training. The training is a very rigorous one because it has to ensure a certain discipline, a certain confidence, and these can come only through suffering. The lot of an instrument must be a hard one, not an easy one. If mediums were to be found without trouble they would not be qualified for their task. The spiritual side of their nature must be tried and tested to see that they can withstand the kind of experience which will profoundly stir them to their highest and deepest possibilities. That is their own equipment; that is their own spiritual armoury.

If they fail to pass through that test then they cannot teach others. You could not be a teacher until you have learned the lessons. And to learn the lessons you must do so in suffering, in travail, in being placed in situations where you may sometimes feel that there is nothing left, no one to whom you can turn. And it is only when you have thus plumbed the depths of spiritual experience that you are qualified by the law of correspondence to rise to the heights of spiritual attainment. This awakening of souls, this bringing of spiritual truths to hungry, thirsty souls, this is very important. This indeed is the whole reason for their existence on earth, but many go through your world without deriving from it the equipment that should be theirs.

When they come here they are unready, or else their minds have been stuffed with so much untruth that they have to unlearn before they can learn anything at all. It is so much easier and more natural for them to learn their lessons in the place where they were intended to learn them, instead of having in our world so many misfits, ill-equipped, unready individuals. It is not possible to be able to comfort the mourners, to help the troubled, the perplexed and the problem-stricken ones unless you yourself have plumbed the depths of sorrow and sadness, till your own soul has so been touched by your own experiences that you are fit to teach others.

The teacher cannot teach until he has learned the lessons himself through the only way that the lessons can be learned. Spiritual lessons cannot be learned vicariously. They must be learned through suffering, through pain, through experience that sometimes seems bitter and hard and very difficult. That is the plan for every instrument who has real service to give. I would sometimes that it were otherwise. But out of all that experience comes a spiritual awareness, a spiritual realisation, a spiritual depth, a profundity that none other can understand, because you learn to place complete and utter faith in the power which upholds you through all doubt and trial until it helps you to bring yourself safely into the haven of a developed soul.

This is a divine pattern instituted as part of the law. The road to spiritual attainment is not an easy one. Were it easy, it would not be attainment. Were it easy then the prize would not be worth having. To give service you have to be ready to serve. And to be ready you yourself must undergo those experiences which will touch your soul, unfold your spirit and put your psychic gifts on the highest possible spiritual level. There are many with psychic gifts, but there are not so many with psychic gifts expressed in any spiritual heights. We are concerned only with those who wish to use the gifts of the spirit, not just the gifts of the astral body, not the extension of the physical senses for experiment, however interesting that may be to scientists and researchers, and I say this in no sense of disparagement. There is work for them to do.

There are many people who want to change your world, who do not wish to change themselves. And there are many people who want to change other people, but all development and all reform must start with the individual soul. Until you yourself have unfolded your spiritual gifts and expressed them and utilised them in service, you are not fit to reform anyone else. We are, of course, concerned with the great task of regeneration, but man must regenerate himself. He must find himself. He must change his own heart, his own mind, his own outlook, so that the spirit which is divine finds the fullest expression.

I do not care what religious label or political label is worn. I do not think that is important. If it helps, that is all right. But what is important is that lives should be lived in the full, divine light, in the rich radiance, in the nobility and dignity which are the gifts of the Great Spirit as part of the heritage of every child. That is greater than any label, than any church, or any religion. The gifts of the spirit are lavish and are freely offered as part of the normal heritage of every individual who comes into your world.

When people come to you, the important thing is that you can touch their souls. To give a message from a loved one is very helpful. It helps the one in our world and the one in your world. But the whole purpose of that upliftment, the whole lesson to be learned from that is that the soul of the one in your world should be touched and made aware of the spiritual realities which are the only eternal standards which exist in the universe. To give a message of comfort is very important. To heal the sick is very important. To work as I am doing is not as important. But the whole aim of our world, and all who return from it, is to quicken the spiritual awareness of the individuals in your world.

And that is the work you are doing. Never mind what the difficulties are. As long as you are faithful to the great trust reposed in all who are instruments you will never fail. The winds may blow, the rains may come down, but you will not be hurt. You will be sheltered and protected until the storms have gone and the sun shines. Immersed as you are in daily problems, it is hard to know all the time how strong, how mighty, is that power of the spirit which uses you for its beneficent purpose. You can only serve. The power that is expressing itself through you is part of the power that fashioned this whole universe, this mighty, stupendous, cosmic universe.

It is the power which fashioned all the planets and stars. It is the power which gave the ocean its tremendous tidal energy. It is the power that gave the variegated hue and perfume to millions of flowers. It is the power that coated with infinite numbers of colours the birds and beasts and fishes. It is the power which breathed into your clay and made it live. This is the power which is using you. It will never fail. And if you provide, by sincerity of desire and willingness to serve, the necessary conditions, it will reach those who are ready to be reached. Have no fear. You are bathed in the radiance of the divine light which always is yours.

Chapter Eleven

YOUR QUESTIONS ANSWERED

Q. *Will there always be another chance for everybody?*
A. Of course! If there were not a second chance, then the universe would not be ruled by divine love and justice. If the story of man ended with the earthly grave, then the world would be full of mistakes, full of people who have never had compensation or even retribution for the life they have lived. The great glory of the knowledge we strive to bring to your world is that life does not end with death, that all who have suffered, that all who have failed, are provided with an opportunity of self-redemption, that the tears of frustration are wiped away in the knowledge of what can be achieved, that all who have desired to enrich their world and failed can add their lustre to mankind's growth.

Life goes on, and in doing so it provides everybody with another chance to express their innate gifts, the gifts that were denied a manifestation on earth; and conversely it provides the means of remedial discipline for those who have foolishly strutted and imagined that they had been able to escape the natural laws that ruled over all. There is no greater justice than divine justice. None cheats it, none thwarts it, all come within the realm of its ordinance. In that knowledge, the kindly and the decent have nothing to fear, it is only those who have been selfish who need be afraid.

. . .

Q. *How does an avowed materialist fare when he passes over?*
A. Your world for too long has been deluded with the idea that the ones who call themselves religious possess a spiritual advantage over their fellows. That is not axiomatic. You are not the spiritual superior of your fellow because you believe in certain theological doctrines. The only test which is applied is the test of daily life. Your spiritual nature is exactly what you have made it to be, and there are many materialists and atheists and rationalists and agnostics who are the spiritual superiors of thousands who think that they are amongst the elect because they have bowed the knee in homage to the Great Spirit and accept certain doctrines. The test is not what you believe, but what you have done, otherwise there would be a complete mockery of divine justice.

. . .

Q. *What is the function of prayer?*
A. If we draw a distinction between selfish requests and true prayer, then we will get an understanding of how the true prayer operates. Obviously selfish requests cannot be called prayers because they have no real value. No one in realms beyond your earth is interested in purely selfish requests that want more possessions, more money or more houses. These will not add one iota to your spiritual nature or increase your mental development.

But there is the true prayer which springs from the soul; the prayer which in itself is a spiritual exercise; the prayer which seeks illumination on the soul's path; the prayer which desires to obtain a closer fusion with the power that is behind all life. In this kind of prayer you have what is the equivalent to a spiritual introspection, for, aware of your shortcomings and imperfections, you are automatically releasing some of the latent energy within yourself and enabling your prayer to have its answer, because you are creating the potency by which the prayer can be fulfilled.

Sometimes I have said that the best answer to many prayers is to disregard them completely, for if the requests were conceded the individuals would be far worse off. But real prayer, that emanates from the soul, that desires greater knowledge, greater understanding, greater strength, that prayer automatically attracts its response. It creates a vibration, and along that vibration can travel the help that is required for the soul who has reached a stage of evolution when he or she is ready for the next step on the path. When a prayer is made in danger you would automatically attract a blanketing power that can protect you and bring those who are your guardians, not only those who are tied to you by links of blood but others who are attracted by love. They can shield you, as many have found, because they have been helped in times of danger.

. . .

Q. Do spirit doctors know the cure for cancer?

A. There is no specific cure in the sense that there is one remedy that will cure every type of cancer, because they do not all owe their origin to the same cause. Some are physical, some are mental and some are spiritual in their origin. It is not possible to treat them all alike. You must try to understand the way we work. It is not done by saying, "Your world has a problem, here is the answer." Your world must earn the answer. But if you have wrong living in your world, if you have the needless cruelty to which helpless animals are subjected, if you have not earned the right to be cured, then no one can give you a cure.

What is done is twofold. Where patently sincere and devoted individuals are working along truly spiritual lines, they are helped automatically because they attract wiser beings who were in their field and who desire to help them. The other method is by the outpouring of spirit power in healing which produces results when the sufferer is ready to receive them. All healing from our world is accomplished through spirit power. It is not a magic wand that can be waved. That power is attracted to the soul of the sufferer. Therefore it cannot induce a response until that soul is touched. There is no magnetic link until the soul is open. If it is closed in, it cannot make any contact. It also depends on other factors, too. It depends on what is the cause of the disease. It depends on the purpose for which that soul is incarnated. It depends whether a choice has been made beforehand to express itself through a certain type of bodily mechanism. It is not a simple question.

. . .

Q. *Is reincarnation true?*

A. This is a very vexed question because always there are differences of opinion in our world amongst those who know, and those who do not know. There are those who are just as emphatic in rejecting the idea of reincarnation as there are those equally emphatic in favouring it because of their experience. I am among the last category because it is something I have experienced. But, as always, it is a confusing question because, as you have heard me say so many times, it is not the same facet of the individuality that reincarnates.

. . .

Q. *Do spirit laws work in the same way in your world as they do in this?*

A. No, they do not work in the same way because ours is a graded life in which the people who have reached the same stage of evolution occupy the same plane of existence. Thus they do not have the comparisons of earth where you have on one plane contrasting experiences. In our world everyone is on the plane to which they have evolved. We cannot have an undeveloped and a highly developed soul in the same sphere of existence. On one surface in your world you meet, day by day, people of differing mental and spiritual attainment. But that is not so in our world, unless we choose to indulge in missionary work and go, comparatively speaking, to lower spheres. Otherwise we meet with our own spiritual equals. When we have evolved, we go on to the next spiritual level. Thus there is not in one sphere the comparisons of existence.

In any case we have no darkness and light, we have no shadows. Those who have reached the attainment where they live in the light of the spirit have the understanding of what the light is, otherwise they could not be there. Those who have not attained that stage are still in the astral belt where they have the illusion of light and dark. As you unfold greater still, you do not require that comparison. You will have a truer understanding of realities and will know the face of truth for what it is.

When you can get the "wholeness" of a flower revealed to you, because you have the spiritual gaze, that gives an appreciation of floral beauty you could not have in your world because we see the "inside" and the "outside" of everything that exists. There is an infinite variation of colour that you do not have in your world. There are varieties of hues and there is spiritual depth which is the reality of substance that cannot be understood with material perception. We are not subject to the gravitational pull of earth and there is eternal light for us. As your soul unfolds, beauty unfolds for it. Ours is a creative world, self-created by those who dwell in it.

. . .

Q. *What is your view of present trends in Spiritualism?*

A. The tide ebbs and flows. There are periods of activity and there are periods of stillness. You cannot maintain any movement by one outburst of energy. On the surface it would seem that so much progress has been made, that tremendous victories have been gained, but, against that, there are millions of people who are completely ignorant of the truths of the spirit. As I have always told you, what you call Spiritualism is only a name. To me, it is the natural law in operation. I am concerned with the spreading of knowledge so that ignorance may be vanquished. I applaud any effort by the individual, or a group, to spread that knowledge.

From what has been revealed to me, I know that the overall plan must succeed. Spirit truth has come to stay in your world. It may be that there are occasional ebbs. It may be that there are periods of enthusiasm and, at other times, indifference. It may be that some grow weary in the task. But this is only a very small part of a large picture. The emphasis in your world is on healing. That is deliberate, not accidental. It is making its mark in a manner that is designed to awaken the consciousness of those who very largely should be bound to realise that spirit power is the reason for their cures, their improvements, their amelioration.

I am never pessimistic with regard to the truths of the spirit. I am always optimistic, because I know the power which is behind us. I rest content in what I have seen. I know that people in your world can hinder, retard or delay, but they cannot stop the advance of spirit truths. That is all that matters. It is part of a tremendous plan. It does not matter what the clergyman says, what the doctor says, or what the scientist says. They have no power to prevent spirit truths from being made known more and more as time goes on in your world.

. . .

Q. *Do they not make mistakes in the spirit world?*
A. Yes! The astral planes are very much like your world. People who live there are very much at a similar stage of development to the average person in your world. They are neither angels nor demons. They are just the ordinary sort of people, not too high, not too low. They make mistakes due to faulty judgments, lack of wisdom, mistakes due to rancour not having been extirpated, to hatred and selfishness, the mistakes that come from imperfection.

. . .

Q. *How can the Creator be all-loving when He has made nature red in tooth and claw?*
A. Finite wisdom cannot comprehend infinite wisdom. You cannot answer the problems of universal activity by viewing them only through physical eyes, or by attempting to understand them with your limited mentalities, limited because you can see only a small fragment of a very large picture. It is, of course, true that in one aspect some animals are predatory and that when they require food they have to be "red in tooth and claw". But it is only a very small

part of the story because there is a principle of harmony and co-operation at work in the animal world as there is in the human world. It is seen when the opportunity is provided for this law of co-operation to outwork itself.

There is also the aspect that man has a responsibility, a great responsibility, towards what is regarded as a lower form of creation, because animals and humans are part of life equally with the tree, the fruit, the flower, the vegetable, the bird. All life moves forward together, or backward together. Thus, if man displays the divine qualities of love, mercy and compassion, then the wolf can lie down with the lamb.

. . .

Q. *Does every human being have a spirit guide?*

A. From the moment of conception, and even before that, there is attached to the incarnating soul someone who volunteers to act as his guardian. "He has given His angels charge concerning thee, to keep thee in Thy ways" is a literal truth. The guardian will maintain to the best of his or her ability the function assumed until the time comes for you to cross the border. The task becomes easier when you are aware of the guardianship; it becomes difficult when you are unaware of it. There is only one guide, but many helpers. The guardian angel knows before he assumes his task what lies ahead of him—and he does not have a free choice in the matter either. Not everyone can say I will be the guardian to this or that person. Ours is a very organised world.

. . .

Q. *Is there any retribution on earth for acts we do?*

A. Sometimes yes, sometimes no. The law does not always

fulfil itself in your world. It does fulfil itself, because it must fulfil itself. Effect and cause cannot be divorced from one another. The time element depends upon the nature of the cause that will produce the effect. Thus there are actions which will produce their reactions whilst you are in your world, but the spiritual results are mechanical in their aftermath. If one does another harm, that harm is registered on the spirit of the doer. Thus his soul is poor by the degree of harm that he has done. Whether that will be shown in his physical life, I do not know. It depends upon the circumstances, but it is measured on his spiritual life which is the eternal life.

. . .

Q. *How would you explain death to a child?*
A. If the child has the ability to understand what is being said, of course, I would say that death is the opening of a door into a larger life, just as the cage is opened to allow the bird to be free.

. . .

Q. *When a small child is stricken with a painful, incurable disease wherein lies the cause? And is this just?*
A. You will not solve spiritual problems with material measurements. You cannot judge eternity by the portion of it that you experience in your very short earthly life. You cannot comprehend divine justice, which is ruled by infinite laws, when you see only one infinitesimal fragment of life at work. How can the lesser comprehend the greater? How can the drop of water judge the ocean? How can the fragment explain the whole?

The universe is ruled by wondrous laws to which I pay constant tribute, for they were conceived by perfect wisdom. They make no mistakes. Sometimes it will seem to you that there is injustice because you only know part of the story. When you see the whole of the story you will change your opinion. You cannot, whilst in earthly life, with its short span, understand infinity.

You cannot know anything of compensation or retribution. You have no means of appreciating the vast richness, beauty and wonder of a spirit life which has no means of offering you any comparisons with what you already know. How then can it be explained to those whose judgments must be limited, whose vision must be restricted, what the other side of the picture is? If you have children born because the physical apparatus is constructed by the parents, then surely it must be apparent that whatever is in the physical make-up of the parents must go into the child's structure. Thus the sins of the parents are visited on the children.

But the child is, by virtue of its birth, a part of the Great Spirit. It has a divine heritage, a latent infinite divinity that can outweigh all physical disadvantages. Matter is not superior to spirit; matter is the servant; spirit is the master. Spiritual growth is a slow but certain process. Spiritual perception and understanding can come only when the soul is ready. To some the truths that we have to preach must fall on deaf ears. It was always so. When the soul is touched, it will be ready to appreciate truths that are waiting for it. You cannot place yourself in the position of the Great Spirit pronouncing judgment.

. . .

Q. *Is the development of psychic faculties the next step in man's evolutionary progress?*

A. Without question, those who are termed psychic, or mediumistic, are the precursors of evolution. They are the advance guard of the next rung in the ladder of evolution. In time to come, psychic faculties will be part of the normal equipment of human beings. Your world is going through a stage of mental unfoldment, and that is why the unfolding psychic faculty will follow in its trail.

You must appreciate that man is not an animal confined to five avenues for his sole contacts with the universe. These five windows allow him to know only a small part of universal activity. They limit him to that which can be registered in terms of matter. Man is more than matter, man is mind and spirit, and there are vibrations that belong to the mental and spiritual life. In addition, there are vibrations which belong to the superphysical life, the life that is beyond the earthly world. Man can register the vibrations of this life in which he lives, and the vibrations of that larger life which one day will be his eternal habitat.

. . .

Q. Is it possible for you to locate any particular individual in your world?

A. It can be done by those who are skilled in the performance of these tasks. You must appreciate that the individuals in our world fall into two categories, those who desire to return and those who do not desire to return. Amongst those who desire to return, it is quite easy to establish contact with your world, provided there is a suitable instrument. Those who do not desire to return can be easily located, but there is nothing that we can do to compel them to return.

. . .

Q. *What is the use of man's earthly experience, bearing in mind it is so limited in comparison with eternity?*

A. Eternity is the sum total of an infinite number of experiences. In eternity, every experience, every action, word and thought plays its part, however small it may be. Eternity is the result of all these accumulated experiences, and if one is lacking then there is not a complete balance. In a vast orchestra of two or three hundred players the man who sounds the triangle, regarded perhaps as the most insignificant instrumentalist, has an important part to play, for if when his time comes he strikes the wrong note, or if he fails to add his sound to the volume, then the whole symphony would be distorted. You realise that. So it is with your earthly lives. It is part, and an essential part, of the training of the soul, and your soul will register indelibly for ever the marks of that training.

Chapter Twelve

POSTSCRIPT

Your world is concerned with bodies. We are concerned with spirits that have to express themselves through bodies. If the spirit is expressing itself properly, all will go well with the body, for matter is always the servant, not the master. Spirit is king and matter is subject.

This truth has illumined your life and made all the difference. You have found yourself. It has brought you knowledge and an understanding that cannot be assessed in earthly language or even material wealth.

This is an abiding truth. The knowledge of this reality is the key that unlocks all the riddles and enables everything to fall into its proper place. It is not what affects the body which is so important but what touches the soul. We can never say to you that no problems will cross your path, no difficulties will arise, or that you will encounter no obstacles or handicaps. That would be untrue.

Earthly life is a struggle in which inner perfection seeks to express itself through imperfection, in which the gold seeks to drive out the dross. Difficulties, problems and obstacles and handicaps are the essential milestones on the road of spiritual unfoldment and attainment. If the prizes of the spirit were easily attained they would not be worth having. Self-discipline, self-mastery, self-illumination, self-unfoldment, these are the prizes to be earned, but no one can come by them easily. There is no royal road.

It is through struggle and strife, through finding light when you have been in the shadows, appreciating the sunshine because you have endured the storm—it is only thus that the soul comes into its own. As correspondingly low as man sinks so correspondingly high can he rise. There could be no Mount of Transfiguration without the Garden of Gethsemane. What happened to the Nazarene is in essence what happens to every human earthly life. Defeat and victory are both essential, for how can you know victory unless you have tasted defeat?

I am trying very hard to put in nutshell form the aphorisms of the spirit which have strict application to daily life. This is not abstruse philosophy. It is very practical spiritual teaching, which teaches you how to derive from life all that it has to offer. The satisfaction is an inner serenity and radiance, an inner tranquillity and confidence because the soul is coming into its own. When the soul is aware of this, you have found yourself and you have found the Great Spirit. Then life's pinpricks will not touch you, for you will have access to that tremendous armoury of the spirit which can sustain you at all times.

There is no problem so great that you do not possess the power to solve it, no burden so heavy that you do not possess the power to carry it. These are truths which I have tried to instil into you and others. Because I know that once they have obtained a lodgement within you, you are so well armed that nothing will daunt you. The power of the spirit is very mighty, but it can flow only where the means allow it to do so. You are the channels.

You give us the channels and we will see that the power flows through you and through others. You give us the willing heart and mind and soul that aspire to serve and you are providing conditions by which that majestic power of the spirit can flow. And as it flows through you, it always leaves behind that deposit, which stimulates your own life. There is nothing in this world of matter that can touch your soul in any way unless you allow it so to do.

You have learnt many lessons and you must learn them, for I cannot learn them for you. The hardest part of our work is to stand aside and watch while those we love fight the battle. I do not mean by standing aside that we do not help them. What we would willingly do is to fight it for them. We must not rob you of your incentive or divest you of the means by which your soul grows.

The Nazarene said that the kingdom of heaven is within. That is a great truth. The Great Spirit is not in some far-off, remote or inaccessible sphere. The Great Spirit is within you and you are within the Great Spirit. Within yourself there are the means for achieving all that is necessary for your own growth and development. That is what you are in your world for.

Because of what I have seen I have an unshakable confidence in the power that rules the universe. I marvel and respect that Intelligence which, with unfailing constancy, and guided by divine love, establishes the whole course of the universe. If only those who live on earth would learn to harmonise themselves with that power, then they could change the whole of the world in which they live. This is all freely offered. There could be nothing more lavish than the bounty which the Great Spirit offers to every child.

Never despair, never be despondent. Try not to worry or to allow anxiety to find a lodgement in your being. Never permit fear to draw close to you. Banish fear, that cold and unwelcome visitor who should never be given admittance to your temple. You have enjoyed momentarily that inner serenity which comes when you have known that you are one with the purpose behind life. Allow that spirit power, which is round and about you, to guide you. It will help you. It will clearly show you the way. When confronted with any problem withdraw from the rush, the bustle, the seething controversy. Withdraw to the silence and allow that power to point the way.

The jewels of the spirit never tarnish or lose their lustre. People who have much of your world's goods do not realise that they are only trustees. To the soul who understands, wealth, like knowledge, brings greater responsibilities. You are an instrument of the greatest power in the universe. You may wear no prelate's robes or have a cardinal's ring on your finger. These are trappings. They have nothing whatever to do with reality. The power of which you are one instrument is greater than all popes, prelates or cardinals. It is the mightiest power of all.

Chapter Thirteen

WHEN A GUIDE PRAYS

Throughout the years Silver Birch has always opened and closed the Hannen Swaffer home circle with a prayer. These have a similarity of theme, but the words are always different. Here is a typical invocation:

"Oh Great White Spirit, who art the genesis of creation, the supreme power, the arbiter of all destiny, we express our gratitude for everything that we have received.

"We are grateful for the light that has illumined the dark places for us, for the knowledge that has made us understand Thee better and also ourselves, for the wisdom that has bathed us with its glory and radiance.

"We are grateful for all that has enabled us to understand the reason for our being, the purpose that lies behind the universe and the love that has constantly guided us.

"We are grateful for all who have made the way possible, the pioneers who have laboured and the reformers who struggled, the teachers, the philosophers, the sages, all who have sought to instruct and to help, some not recognised in their earthly day and others still unknown.

"We are grateful for all the richness that has been showered upon us. We raise our voices in thankfulness and ask that we may indeed be worthy and inspired so to order our lives that we in our turn can be Thy channels, helping to fulfil Thy purpose and serve those less fortunate than ourselves.

"This is the prayer of Thy Indian servant who seeks always to serve."